The PRESIDENTS
of the United States of America

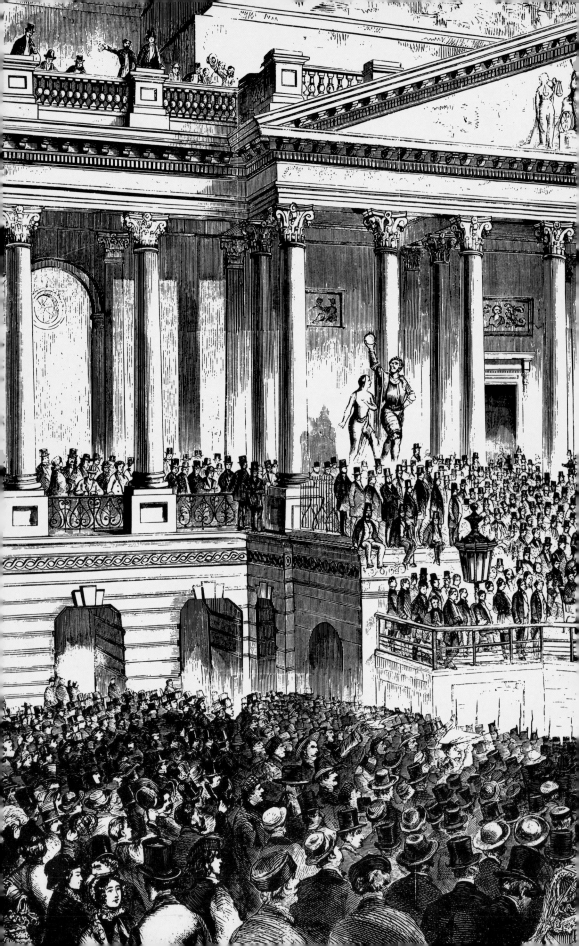

THE
PRESIDENTS
OF
THE UNITED STATES
OF AMERICA

BY FRANK FREIDEL

Professor of History
Harvard University

WHITE HOUSE HISTORICAL ASSOCIATION

with the cooperation of the National Geographic Society

WASHINGTON, D. C.

Published by the WHITE HOUSE HISTORICAL ASSOCIATION, *5026 New Executive Office
Building, 726 Jackson Place, N.W., Washington, D. C. 20506*

Produced by the National Geographic Society as a public service.

FRANC SHOR, *Editorial Director;* ROBERT L. BREEDEN, *Project Editor.*

Editorial and research staff: WAYNE BARRETT, BART McDOWELL, MARY ANN
HARRELL, ABIGAIL T. BRETT, LEDLIE L. DINSMORE, MARGARET LADD, WERNER
JANNEY, DONALD J. CRUMP, MARGARET S. DEAN, *and* DOROTHY CORSON.

Staff for revised edition: PHILIP B. SILCOTT, CLETIS PRIDE, SUSAN BURNS, JANE H.
BUXTON, JUNE L. GRAHAM, RAJA D. MURSHED, JENNIFER C. URQUHART, *and* GEORGE
V. WHITE.

Photographs of the Presidential portraits by GEORGE F. MOBLEY *and* VICTOR R. BOSWELL, JR.

Production and printing: ROBERT W. MESSER, JAMES
R. WHITNEY, JOHN R. METCALFE, JOHN L. McINTOSH.

Sixth Edition, Second Printing, Library of Congress catalog number 64-66269

FRONTISPIECE: GEORGE WASHINGTON *takes the oath of office which
every Chief Executive since that April day in 1789 has sworn to
uphold. Washington stands on the balcony of a Wall Street building
in New York City, then the Nation's capital.*

FRONT ENDSHEET: ABRAHAM LINCOLN *in 1861 addresses an inaugural crowd
beneath the unfinished Capitol dome. As a divided Nation faced the
"momentous issue of civil war," he took "the most solemn" oath
"to preserve, protect and defend the Constitution of the United States."*

BACK ENDSHEET: THE PRESIDENT'S HOUSE *in its pastoral setting of the
1820's appears in this old English engraving as Presidents John Quincy
Adams and Andrew Jackson knew it.*

Foreword

HISTORY IS THE STUDY of people, ideas, events, and their interaction over the years. These elements have rarely combined more forcefully and dramatically than in the Presidency of the United States. Each Administration is a unique study in the politics, diplomacy, economy, and personalities of an individual epoch; each President is the study of how one man, from the singular vantage point of the White House, shaped or guided these vital and often conflicting forces. Some succeeded better than others; all did their best.

This volume, researched and written to meet the high standards of the National Geographic Society, faithfully recounts the histories of the 37 men privileged to have served as President of the United States. By capturing the spirit of each time, and the character of each President, the work serves as a kind of family album of the American people. The men who occupied the Presidency reflect the richness and diversity of American life as it evolved over the years. Country squires like Washington and Jefferson, humble sons of the soil like Lincoln and Jackson, lawyers, soldiers, civil servants, farmers, and scholars—every President has become part of the rich tapestry of American history and each has brought a different blend of strengths, weaknesses, and personal touches to our highest office.

To some of them, their years in the White House were an ordeal. President Buchanan went so far as to call the Presidency a "crown of thorns." Others found the Presidency exhilarating. "No President ever enjoyed himself in the Presidency as much as I did," Theodore Roosevelt declared. In the next generation, his kinsman, Franklin D. Roosevelt, who served longer in office than any other President, would quip at a news conference that "the first twelve years are the hardest."

Harry Truman, who once likened the job to riding on a tiger, also left behind a simple but crucial rule of thumb for those who came after him. "A President," he warned, "if he is to have clear perspective and never get out of touch, must cut through the voices around him, know his history, and make certain of the reliability of the information he gets."

It is this contact—this understanding, living link with the American people and the American experience—that has marked all of our great leaders. It was a quality which they had when they came to the Presidency, and which they strengthened as they grew in the office.

Perhaps this was best expressed by a man I came to know and greatly respect while I served in the Congress and he in the White House. Dwight D. Eisenhower was a small-town boy from Abilene, Kansas, who had already earned fame as a wartime military leader. Then, in 1952, the Nation called him to the Presidency. It was a new job, with different challenges. And, in filling it, Ike managed to *grow* without changing— without losing his basic character and values. This is how he explained it, in words I will always remember:

"My role may have changed but I have not changed. All my life I have said what I meant and meant what I said. No one will change that. All my life I had a deep and fundamental faith in my country, in its people, in its principles and in its spiritual value. No one will change that."

This same immutable faith was shared by Washington, by Lincoln, and by all of the men whom we now remember as great Presidents. In every time of crisis that faith has also been shared by the American people. It is still alive today as we approach our third century as a Nation. It forms a living bridge between us and all of the ideals and adventures that have unfolded in the heroic pages of American history. Its story is part of our lives and we, in our turn, are writing a new chapter in the story itself.

Gerald R. Ford

Contents

Official White House portraits by the artists indicated above appear opposite Presidential biographies. The photographs of Richard M. Nixon and Gerald R. Ford are included because official paintings have not been commissioned.

ACKNOWLEDGEMENT: THE DIRECTORS OF THE WHITE HOUSE HISTORICAL ASSOCIATION ARE GRATEFUL TO THE NATIONAL GEOGRAPHIC SOCIETY, ESPECIALLY TO DR. MELVIN M. PAYNE, PRESIDENT, AND DR. MELVILLE BELL GROSVENOR, EDITOR-IN-CHIEF, FOR PROVIDING, AS A PUBLIC SERVICE, THE PHOTOGRAPHIC AND EDITORIAL STAFFS FOR THIS BOOK.

ON APRIL 30, 1789, George Washington, standing on the balcony of Federal Hall on Wall Street in New York, took his oath of office as the first President of the United States. "As the first of every thing, *in our situation* will serve to establish a Precedent," he wrote James Madison, "it is devoutly wished on my part, that these precedents may be fixed on true principles."

Born in 1732 into a Virginia planter family, he learned the morals, manners, and body of knowledge requisite for an 18th-century Virginia gentleman.

He pursued two intertwined interests: military arts and western expansion. At 16 he helped survey Shenandoah lands for Thomas, Lord Fairfax. Commissioned a lieutenant colonel in 1754, he fought the first skirmishes of what grew into the French and Indian War. The next year, as an aide to Gen. Edward Braddock, he escaped injury although four bullets ripped his coat and two horses were shot from under him.

From 1759 to the outbreak of the American Revolution, Washington managed his lands around Mount Vernon and served in the Virginia House of Burgesses. Married to a widow, Martha Dandridge Custis, he devoted himself to a busy and happy life. But like his fellow planters, Washington felt himself exploited by British merchants and hampered by British regulations. As the quarrel with the mother country grew acute, he moderately but firmly voiced his resistance to the restrictions.

When the Second Continental Congress assembled in Philadelphia in May, 1775, Washington, one of the Virginia delegates, was elected Commander in Chief of the Continental Army. On July 3, 1775, at Cambridge, Massachusetts, he took command of his ill-trained troops and embarked upon a war that was to last six grueling years.

He realized early that the best strategy was to harass the British. He reported to Congress, "we should on all Occasions avoid a general Action, or put anything to the Risque, unless compelled by a necessity, into which we ought never to be drawn." Ensuing battles saw him fall back slowly, then strike unexpectedly. Finally in 1781—with the aid of French allies—he forced the surrender of Cornwallis at Yorktown.

Washington longed to retire to his fields at Mount Vernon. But he soon realized that the Nation under its Articles of Confederation was not functioning well, so he became a prime mover in the steps leading to the Constitutional Convention at Philadelphia in 1787. When the new Constitution was ratified, the Electoral College unanimously elected Washington President.

He did not infringe upon the policy-making powers that he felt the Constitution gave Congress. But the determination of foreign policy became preponderantly a Presidential concern. When the French Revolution led to a major war between France and England, Washington refused to accept entirely the recommendations of either his Secretary of State Thomas Jefferson, who was pro-French, or his Secretary of the Treasury Alexander Hamilton, who was pro-British. Rather, he insisted upon a neutral course until the United States could grow stronger.

To his disappointment, two parties were developing by the end of his first term. Wearied of politics, feeling old, he retired at the end of his second. In his Farewell Address, he urged his countrymen to forswear excessive party spirit and geographical distinctions. In foreign affairs, he warned against long-term alliances.

Washington enjoyed less than three years of retirement at Mount Vernon, for he died of a throat infection December 14, 1799. For months the Nation mourned him.

George Washington's integrity set a pattern for all other Presidents to follow.

John Adams

SECOND PRESIDENT 1797-1801

LEARNED and thoughtful, John Adams was more remarkable as a political philosopher than as a politician. "People and nations are forged in the fires of adversity," he said, doubtless thinking of his own as well as the American experience.

Adams was born in the Massachusetts Bay Colony in 1735. A Harvard-educated lawyer, he early became identified with the patriot cause; a delegate to the First and Second Continental Congresses, he led in the movement for independence.

During the Revolutionary War he served in France and Holland in diplomatic roles, and helped negotiate the treaty of peace. From 1785 to 1788 he was minister to the Court of St. James's, returning to be elected Vice President under George Washington.

Adams's two terms as Vice President were frustrating experiences for a man of his vigor, intellect, and vanity. He complained to his wife Abigail, "My country has in its wisdom contrived for me the most insignificant office that ever the invention of man contrived or his imagination conceived."

When Adams became President, the war between the French and British was causing great difficulties for the United States on the high seas and intense partisanship among contending factions within the Nation.

His administration focused on France, where the Directory, the ruling group, had refused to receive the American envoy and had suspended commercial relations.

Adams sent three commissioners to France, but in the spring of 1798 word arrived that the French Foreign Minister Talleyrand and the Directory had refused to negotiate with them unless they would first pay a substantial bribe. Adams reported the insult to Congress, and the Senate printed the correspondence, in which the Frenchmen were referred to only as "X, Y, and Z."

The Nation broke out into what Jefferson called "the X. Y. Z. fever," increased in intensity by Adams's exhortations. The populace cheered itself hoarse wherever the President appeared. Never had the Federalists been so popular.

Congress appropriated money to complete three new frigates and to build additional ships, and authorized the raising of a provisional army. It also passed the Alien and Sedition Acts, intended to frighten foreign agents out of the country and to stifle the attacks of Republican editors.

President Adams did not call for a declaration of war, but hostilities began at sea. At first, American shipping was almost defenseless against French privateers, but by 1800 armed merchantmen and U. S. warships were clearing the sea lanes.

Despite several brilliant naval victories, war fever subsided. Word came to Adams that France also had no stomach for war and would receive an envoy with respect. Long negotiations ended the quasi war.

Sending a peace mission to France brought the full fury of the Hamiltonians against Adams. In the campaign of 1800 the Republicans were united and effective, the Federalists badly divided. Nevertheless, Adams polled only a few less electoral votes than Jefferson, who became President.

On November 1, 1800, just before the election, Adams arrived in the new Capital City to take up his residence in the White House. On his second evening in its damp, unfinished rooms, he wrote his wife, "Before I end my letter, I pray Heaven to bestow the best of Blessings on this House and all that shall hereafter inhabit it. May none but honest and wise Men ever rule under this roof."

Adams retired to his farm in Quincy. Here he penned his elaborate letters to Thomas Jefferson. Here, on July 4, 1826, he whispered his last words: "Thomas Jefferson survives." But Jefferson had died at Monticello a few hours earlier.

John Adams, a shaper of the Revolution, saved his Nation from war with France.

Th Jefferson (signature)

THIRD PRESIDENT 1801-1809

IN THE THICK of party conflict in 1800, Thomas Jefferson wrote in a private letter, "I have sworn upon the altar of God eternal hostility against every form of tyranny over the mind of man."

This powerful advocate of liberty was born in 1743 in Albemarle County, Virginia, inheriting from his father, a planter and surveyor, some 5,000 acres of land, and from his mother, a Randolph, high social standing. He studied at the College of William and Mary, then read law. In 1772 he married Martha Wayles Skelton, a widow, and took her to live in his partly constructed mountaintop home, Monticello.

Freckled and sandy-haired, rather tall and awkward, Jefferson was eloquent as a correspondent, but he was no public speaker. In the Virginia House of Burgesses and the Continental Congress, he contributed his pen rather than his voice to the patriot cause. As the "silent member" of the Congress, Jefferson, at 33, drafted the Declaration of Independence. In years following he labored to make its words a reality in Virginia. Most notably, he wrote a bill establishing religious freedom, enacted in 1786.

Jefferson succeeded Benjamin Franklin as minister to France in 1785. His sympathy for the French Revolution led him into conflict with Alexander Hamilton when Jefferson was Secretary of State in President Washington's Cabinet. He resigned in 1793.

Sharp political conflict developed, and two separate parties, the Federalists and the Democratic-Republicans, began to form. Jefferson gradually assumed leadership of the Republicans, who sympathized with the revolutionary cause in France. Attacking Federalist policies, he opposed a strong centralized government and championed the rights of states.

As a reluctant candidate for President in 1796, Jefferson came within three votes of election. Through a flaw in the Constitution, he became Vice President, although an opponent of President Adams. In 1800 the defect caused a more serious problem. Republican electors, attempting to name both a President and a Vice President from their own party, cast a tie vote between Jefferson and Aaron Burr. The House of Representatives settled the tie. Hamilton, disliking both Jefferson and Burr, nevertheless urged Jefferson's election.

When Jefferson assumed the Presidency, the crises in France had passed. He slashed Army and Navy expenditures, cut the budget, eliminated the tax on whiskey so unpopular in the West, yet reduced the national debt by a third. He also sent a naval squadron to fight the Barbary pirates, harassing American commerce in the Mediterranean. Further, although the Constitution made no provision for the acquisition of new land, Jefferson suppressed his qualms over constitutionality when he had the opportunity to acquire the Louisiana Territory from Napoleon in 1803.

During Jefferson's second term, he was increasingly preoccupied with keeping the Nation from involvement in the Napoleonic wars, though both England and France interfered with the neutral rights of American merchantmen. Jefferson's attempted solution, an embargo upon American shipping, worked badly and was unpopular.

Jefferson retired to Monticello to ponder such projects as his grand designs for the University of Virginia. A French nobleman observed that he had placed his house and his mind "on an elevated situation, from which he might contemplate the universe." He died on July 4, 1826.

Thomas Jefferson gained the immense Louisiana Territory for the infant Republic.

James Madison

FOURTH PRESIDENT 1809-1817

AT HIS INAUGURATION, James Madison, a small, wizened man, appeared old and worn; Washington Irving described him as "but a withered little apple-John." But whatever his deficiencies in charm, Madison's buxom wife Dolley compensated for them with her warmth and gaiety. She was the toast of Washington.

Born in 1751, Madison was brought up in Orange County, Virginia, and attended Princeton (then called the College of New Jersey). A student of history and government, well-read in law, he participated in the framing of the Virginia Constitution in 1776, served in the Continental Congress, and was leader in the Virginia Assembly.

When delegates to the Constitutional Convention assembled at Philadelphia, the 36-year-old Madison took frequent and emphatic part in the debates.

Madison made a major contribution to the ratification of the Constitution by writing, with Alexander Hamilton and John Jay, the *Federalist* essays. In later years, when he was referred to as the "Father of the Constitution," Madison protested that the document was not "the off-spring of a single brain," but "the work of many heads and many hands."

In Congress, he helped frame the Bill of Rights and enact the first revenue legislation. Out of his leadership in opposition to Hamilton's financial proposals, which he felt would unduly bestow wealth and power upon northern financiers, came the development of the Republican, or Jeffersonian, Party.

As President Jefferson's Secretary of State, Madison protested to warring France and Britain that their seizure of American ships was contrary to international law. The protests, John Randolph acidly commented, had the effect of "a shilling pamphlet hurled against eight hundred ships of war."

Despite the unpopular Embargo Act of 1807, which did not make the belligerent nations change their ways but did cause a depression in the United States, Madison was elected President in 1808. Before he took office the Embargo Act was repealed.

During the first year of Madison's Administration, the United States prohibited trade with both Britain and France; then in May, 1810, Congress authorized trade with both, directing the President, if either would accept America's view of neutral rights, to forbid trade with the other nation.

Napoleon pretended to comply, and late in 1810, Madison proclaimed non-intercourse with Great Britain. In Congress a young group including Henry Clay and John C. Calhoun, the "War Hawks," pressed the President for a more militant policy.

The British impressment of American seamen and the seizure of cargoes impelled Madison to give in to the pressure. On June 1, 1812, he asked Congress to declare war.

The young Nation was not prepared to fight; its forces took a severe trouncing. The British entered Washington and set fire to the White House and the Capitol.

But a few notable naval and military victories, climaxed by Gen. Andrew Jackson's triumph at New Orleans, convinced Americans that the War of 1812 had been gloriously successful. An upsurge of nationalism resulted. The New England Federalists who had opposed the war—and who had even talked secession—were so thoroughly repudiated that Federalism disappeared as a national party.

In retirement at Montpelier, his estate in Orange County, Virginia, Madison spoke out against the disruptive states' rights influences that by the 1830's threatened to shatter the Federal Union. In a note opened after his death in 1836, he stated, "The advice nearest to my heart and deepest in my convictions is that the Union of the States be cherished and perpetuated."

James Madison, "Father of the Constitution," led the inconclusive War of 1812.

James Monroe

FIFTH PRESIDENT 1817-1825

ON NEW YEAR'S DAY, 1825, at the last of his annual White House receptions, President James Monroe made a pleasing impression upon a Virginia lady who shook his hand:

"He is tall and well formed. His dress plain and in the old style. . . . His manner was quiet and dignified. From the frank, honest expression of his eye . . . I think he well deserves the encomium passed upon him by the great Jefferson, who said, 'Monroe was so honest that if you turned his soul inside out there would not be a spot on it.' "

Born in Westmoreland County, Virginia, in 1758, Monroe attended the College of William and Mary, fought with distinction in the Continental Army, and practiced law in Fredericksburg, Virginia.

As a youthful politician, he joined the anti-Federalists in the Virginia Convention which ratified the Constitution, and in 1790, an advocate of Jeffersonian policies, was elected United States Senator. As Minister to France in 1794-1796, he displayed strong sympathies for the French cause; later, with Robert R. Livingston, he helped negotiate the Louisiana Purchase.

His ambition and energy, together with the backing of President Madison, made him the Republican choice for the Presidency in 1816. With little Federalist opposition, he easily won re-election in 1820.

Monroe made unusually strong Cabinet choices, naming a southerner, John C. Calhoun, as Secretary of War, and a northerner, John Quincy Adams, as Secretary of State. Only Henry Clay's refusal kept Monroe from adding an outstanding westerner.

Early in his administration, Monroe undertook a goodwill tour. At Boston, his visit was hailed as the beginning of an "Era of Good Feelings." Unfortunately these "good feelings" did not endure, although Monroe, his popularity undiminished, followed nationalist policies.

Across the façade of nationalism, ugly sectional cracks appeared. A painful economic depression undoubtedly increased the dismay of the people of the Missouri Territory in 1819 when their application for admission to the Union as a slave state failed. An amended bill for gradually eliminating slavery in Missouri precipitated two years of bitter debate in Congress.

The Missouri Compromise bill resolved the struggle, pairing Missouri as a slave state with Maine, a free state, and barring slavery north and west of Missouri forever.

In foreign affairs Monroe proclaimed the fundamental policy that bears his name, responding to the threat that the more conservative governments in Europe might try to aid Spain in winning back her former Latin American colonies. Monroe did not begin formally to recognize the young sister republics until 1822, after ascertaining that Congress would vote appropriations for diplomatic missions. He and Secretary of State John Quincy Adams wished to avoid trouble with Spain until it had ceded the Floridas, as was done in 1821.

Great Britain, with its powerful navy, also opposed reconquest of Latin America and suggested that the United States join in proclaiming "hands off." Ex-Presidents Jefferson and Madison counseled Monroe to accept the offer, but Secretary Adams advised, "It would be more candid . . . to avow our principles explicitly to Russia and France, than to come in as a cock-boat in the wake of the British man-of-war."

Monroe accepted Adams's advice. Not only must Latin America be left alone, he warned, but also Russia must not encroach southward on the Pacific coast. ". . . the American continents," he stated, "by the free and independent condition which they have assumed and maintain, are henceforth not to be considered as subjects for future colonization by any European Power." Some 20 years after Monroe died in 1831, this became known as the Monroe Doctrine.

James Monroe declared the Americas no longer subject to European colonization.

John Quincy Adams.

SIXTH PRESIDENT 1825-1829

THE ONLY PRESIDENT who was the son of a President, John Quincy Adams in many respects paralleled the career as well as the temperament and viewpoints of his illustrious father. Born in Braintree, Massachusetts, in 1767, he watched the Battle of Bunker Hill from the top of Penn's Hill above the family farm. As secretary to his father in Europe, he became an accomplished linguist and assiduous diarist.

After graduating from Harvard College, he became a lawyer. At age 26 he was appointed Minister to the Netherlands, then promoted to the Berlin Legation. In 1802 he was elected to the United States Senate. Six years later President Madison appointed him Minister to Russia.

Serving under President Monroe, Adams was one of America's great Secretaries of State, arranging with England for the joint occupation of the Oregon country, obtaining from Spain the cession of the Floridas, and formulating with the President the Monroe Doctrine.

In the political tradition of the early 19th century, Adams as Secretary of State was considered the political heir to the Presidency. But the old ways of choosing a President were giving way in 1824 before the clamor for a popular choice.

Within the one and only party—the Republican—sectionalism and factionalism were developing, and each section put up its own candidate for the Presidency. Adams, the candidate of the North, fell behind Gen. Andrew Jackson in both popular and electoral votes, but received more than William H. Crawford and Henry Clay. Since no candidate had a majority of electoral votes, the election was decided among the top three by the House of Representatives. Clay, who favored a program similar to that of Adams, threw his crucial support in the House to the New Englander.

Upon becoming President, Adams appointed Clay as Secretary of State. Jackson and his angry followers charged that a "corrupt bargain" had taken place and immediately began their campaign to wrest the Presidency from Adams in 1828.

Well aware that he would face hostility in Congress, Adams nevertheless proclaimed in his first Annual Message a spectacular national program. He proposed that the Federal Government bring the sections together with a network of highways and canals, and that it develop and conserve the public domain, using funds from the sale of public lands. In 1828, he broke ground for the 185-mile C & O Canal.

Adams also urged the United States to take a lead in the development of the arts and sciences through the establishment of a national university, the financing of scientific expeditions, and the erection of an observatory. His critics declared such measures transcended constitutional limitations.

The campaign of 1828, in which his Jacksonian opponents charged him with corruption and public plunder, was an ordeal Adams did not easily bear. After his defeat he returned to Massachusetts, expecting to spend the remainder of his life enjoying his farm and his books.

Unexpectedly, in 1830, the Plymouth district elected him to the House of Representatives, and there for the remainder of his life he served as a powerful leader. Above all, he fought against circumscription of civil liberties.

In 1836 southern Congressmen passed a "gag rule" providing that the House automatically table petitions against slavery. Adams tirelessly fought the rule for eight years until finally he obtained its repeal.

In 1848, he collapsed on the floor of the House from a stroke and was carried to the Speaker's Room, where two days later he died. He was buried—as were his father, mother, and wife—at First Parish Church in Quincy. To the end, "Old Man Eloquent" had fought for what he considered right.

John Quincy Adams: the only son of a President to serve as President himself.

Andrew Jackson

SEVENTH PRESIDENT 1829-1837

M ORE NEARLY than any of his predecessors, Andrew Jackson was elected by popular vote; as President he sought to act as the direct representative of the common man.

Born in a backwoods settlement in the Carolinas in 1767, he received sporadic education. But in his late teens he read law for about two years, and he became an outstanding young lawyer in Tennessee. Fiercely jealous of his honor, he engaged in brawls, and in a duel killed a man who cast an unjustified slur on his wife Rachel.

He prospered sufficiently to buy slaves and to build a mansion, the Hermitage, near Nashville. He was the first man elected from Tennessee to the House of Representatives, and he served briefly in the Senate.

A major general in the War of 1812, Jackson became a national hero when he defeated the British at New Orleans.

In 1824 some state political factions rallied around Jackson; by 1828 enough had joined "Old Hickory" to win numerous state elections and control of the Federal administration in Washington.

In his first Annual Message to Congress, Jackson recommended eliminating the Electoral College. He also tried to democratize Federal officeholding. Already state machines were being built on patronage, and a New York Senator openly proclaimed "that to the victors belong the spoils. . . ."

Jackson took a milder view. Decrying officeholders who seemed to enjoy life tenure, he believed Government duties could be "so plain and simple" that offices should rotate among deserving applicants.

As national politics polarized around Jackson and his opposition, two parties grew out of the old Republican Party—the Democratic Republicans, or Democrats, adhering to Jackson; and the National Republicans, or Whigs, opposing him.

Henry Clay, Daniel Webster, and other Whig leaders proclaimed themselves defenders of popular liberties against the usurpation of Jackson. Hostile cartoonists portrayed him as King Andrew I.

Behind their accusations lay the fact that Jackson, unlike previous Presidents, did not defer to Congress in policy-making but used his power of the veto and his party leadership to assume command.

The greatest party battle centered around the Second Bank of the United States, a private corporation but virtually a Government-sponsored monopoly. When Jackson appeared hostile toward it, the Bank threw its power against him.

Clay and Webster, who had acted as attorneys for the Bank, led the fight for its recharter in Congress. "The bank," Jackson told Martin Van Buren, "is trying to kill me, *but I will kill it!*" Jackson, in vetoing the recharter bill, charged the Bank with undue economic privilege.

His views won approval from the American electorate; in 1832 he polled more than 56 percent of the popular vote and almost five times as many electoral votes as Clay.

Jackson met head-on the challenge of John C. Calhoun, leader of forces trying to rid themselves of a high protective tariff.

When South Carolina undertook to nullify the tariff, Jackson ordered armed forces to Charleston and privately threatened to hang Calhoun. Violence seemed imminent until Clay negotiated a compromise: tariffs were lowered and South Carolina dropped nullification.

In January 1832, while the President was dining with friends at the White House, someone whispered to him that the Senate had rejected the nomination of Martin Van Buren as Minister to England. Jackson jumped to his feet and exclaimed, "By the Eternal! I'll smash them!" So he did. His favorite, Van Buren, became Vice President, and succeeded to the Presidency when "Old Hickory" retired to the Hermitage, where he died in June 1845.

Andrew Jackson, first frontier President, came to office with great popular support.

Van Buren (signature)

EIGHTH PRESIDENT 1837-1841

ONLY ABOUT 5 feet, 6 inches tall, but trim and erect, Martin Van Buren dressed fastidiously. His impeccable appearance belied his amiability—and his humble background. Of Dutch descent, he was born in 1782, the son of a tavernkeeper and farmer, in Kinderhook, New York.

As a young lawyer he became involved in New York politics. As leader of the "Albany Regency," an effective New York political organization, he shrewdly dispensed public offices and bounty in a fashion calculated to bring votes. Yet he faithfully fulfilled official duties, and in 1821 was elected to the United States Senate.

By 1827 he had emerged as the principal northern leader for Andrew Jackson. President Jackson rewarded Van Buren by appointing him Secretary of State. As the Cabinet Members appointed at John C. Calhoun's recommendation began to demonstrate only secondary loyalty to Jackson, Van Buren emerged as the President's most trusted adviser. Jackson referred to him as "a *true man* with no guile."

The rift in the Cabinet became serious because of Jackson's differences with Calhoun, a Presidential aspirant. Van Buren suggested a way out of an eventual impasse: he and Secretary of War Eaton resigned, so that Calhoun men would also resign. Jackson appointed a new Cabinet, and sought again to reward Van Buren by appointing him Minister to Great Britain. Vice President Calhoun, as President of the Senate, cast the deciding vote against the appointment—and made a martyr of Van Buren.

The "Little Magician" was elected Vice President on the Jacksonian ticket in 1832, and won the Presidency in 1836.

Van Buren devoted his Inaugural Address to a discourse upon the American experiment as an example to the rest of the world. The country was prosperous, but less than three months later the panic of 1837 punctured the prosperity.

Basically the trouble was the 19th-century cyclical economy of "boom and bust," which was following its regular pattern, but Jackson's financial measures contributed to the crash. His destruction of the Second Bank of the United States had removed restrictions upon the inflationary practices of some state banks; wild speculation in lands, based on easy bank credit, had swept the West. To end this speculation, Jackson in 1836 had issued a Specie Circular requiring that lands be purchased with hard money—gold or silver.

In 1837 the panic began. Hundreds of banks and businesses failed. Thousands lost their lands. For about five years the United States was wracked by the worst depression thus far in its history.

Programs applied decades later to alleviate economic crisis eluded both Van Buren and his opponents. Van Buren's remedy—continuing Jackson's deflationary policies—only deepened and prolonged the depression.

Declaring that the panic was due to recklessness in business and overexpansion of credit, Van Buren devoted himself to maintaining the solvency of the national government. He opposed not only the creation of a new Bank of the United States but also the placing of Government funds in state banks. He fought for the establishment of an independent treasury system to handle Government transactions. As for Federal aid to internal improvements, he cut off expenditures so completely that the Government even sold the tools it had used on public works.

Inclined more and more to oppose the expansion of slavery, Van Buren blocked the annexation of Texas because it assuredly would add to slave territory—and it might bring war with Mexico.

Defeated by the Whigs in 1840 for reelection, he was an unsuccessful candidate for President on the Free Soil ticket in 1848. He died in 1862.

Martin Van Buren was the first Chief Executive born under the United States flag.

W H Harrison

NINTH PRESIDENT 1841

"GIVE HIM A BARREL of hard cider and settle a pension of two thousand a year on him, and my word for it," a Democratic newspaper foolishly gibed, "he will sit . . . by the side of a 'sea coal' fire, and study moral philosophy." The Whigs, seizing on this political misstep, in 1840 presented their candidate William Henry Harrison as a simple frontier Indian fighter, living in a log cabin and drinking cider, in contrast to an aristocratic champagne-sipping Van Buren.

Harrison was in fact a scion of the Virginia planter aristocracy. He was born at Berkeley in 1773. He studied classics and history at Hampden-Sidney College, then began the study of medicine in Richmond.

Suddenly, that same year, 1791, Harrison switched interests. He obtained a commission as ensign in the First Infantry of the Regular Army, and headed to the Northwest, where he spent much of his life.

In the campaign against the Indians, Harrison served as aide-de-camp to General "Mad Anthony" Wayne at the Battle of Fallen Timbers, which opened most of the Ohio area to settlement. After resigning from the Army in 1798, he became Secretary of the Northwest Territory, was its first delegate to Congress, and helped obtain legislation dividing the Territory into the Northwest and Indiana Territories. In 1801 he became Governor of the Indiana Territory, serving 12 years.

His prime task as governor was to obtain title to Indian lands so settlers could press forward into the wilderness. When the Indians retaliated, Harrison was responsible for defending the settlements.

The threat against the settlers became serious in 1809 when an eloquent and energetic chieftain, Tecumseh, with his religious brother, the Prophet, began to strengthen an Indian confederation to prevent further encroachment. In 1811 Harrison received permission to attack the confederacy.

While Tecumseh was away seeking more allies, Harrison led about a thousand men toward the Prophet's town. Suddenly, before dawn on November 7, the Indians attacked his camp on Tippecanoe River. After heavy fighting, Harrison repulsed them, but lost 190 dead and wounded.

The Battle of Tippecanoe, upon which Harrison's fame was to rest, disrupted Tecumseh's confederacy but failed to diminish Indian raids. By the spring of 1812, they were again terrorizing the frontier.

In the War of 1812 Harrison won more military laurels when he was given the command of the Army in the Northwest with the rank of brigadier general. At the Battle of the Thames, north of Lake Erie, on October 5, 1813, he defeated the combined British and Indian forces, and killed Tecumseh. The Indians scattered, never again to offer serious resistance in what was then called the Northwest.

Thereafter Harrison returned to civilian life; the Whigs, in need of a national hero, nominated him for President in 1840. He won by a majority of less than 150,000, but swept the Electoral College, 234 to 60.

When he arrived in Washington in February, 1841, Harrison let Daniel Webster edit his Inaugural Address, ornate with classical allusions. Webster obtained some deletions, boasting in a jolly fashion that he had killed "seventeen Roman proconsuls as dead as smelts, every one of them."

Webster had reason to be pleased, for while Harrison was nationalistic in his outlook, he emphasized in his Inaugural that he would be obedient to the will of the people as expressed through Congress.

But before he had been in office a month, he caught a cold that developed into pneumonia. On April 4, 1841, he died—the first President to die in office—and with him died the Whig program.

William Henry Harrison was the first President to die in office.

John Tyler

TENTH PRESIDENT 1841-1845

DUBBED "HIS ACCIDENCY" by his detractors, John Tyler was the first Vice President to be elevated to the office of President by the death of his predecessor.

Born in Virginia in 1790, he was raised believing that the Constitution must be strictly construed. He never wavered from this conviction. He attended the College of William and Mary and studied law.

Serving in the House of Representatives from 1816 to 1821, Tyler voted against most nationalist legislation and opposed the Missouri Compromise. After leaving the House he served twice as Governor of Virginia. As a Senator he reluctantly supported Jackson for President as a choice of evils. Tyler soon joined the states' rights southerners in Congress who banded with Henry Clay, Daniel Webster, and their newly formed Whig party opposing President Jackson.

The Whigs nominated Tyler for Vice President in 1840, hoping for support from southern states'-righters who could not stomach Jacksonian Democracy. The slogan "Tippecanoe and Tyler Too" implied flag-waving nationalism plus a dash of southern sectionalism.

Clay, intending to keep party leadership in his own hands, minimized his nationalist views temporarily; Webster proclaimed himself "a Jeffersonian Democrat." But after the election, both men tried to dominate "Old Tippecanoe."

Suddenly President Harrison was dead, and "Tyler too" was in the White House. At first the Whigs were not too disturbed, although Tyler insisted upon assuming the full powers of a duly-elected President. He even delivered an Inaugural Address, but it seemed full of good Whig doctrine. Whigs, optimistic that Tyler would accept their program, soon were disillusioned.

Tyler was ready to compromise on the banking question, but Clay would not budge. He would not accept Tyler's "exchequer system," and Tyler vetoed Clay's bill to establish a National Bank with branches in several states. A similar bank bill was passed by Congress. But again, on states' rights grounds, Tyler vetoed it.

In retaliation, the Whigs expelled Tyler from their party. All the Cabinet resigned but Secretary of State Webster.

A year later when Tyler vetoed a tariff bill, the first impeachment resolution against a President was introduced in the House of Representatives. A committee headed by Representative John Quincy Adams reported that the President had misused the veto power, but the resolution failed.

Despite their differences, President Tyler and the Whig Congress enacted much positive legislation. The "Log-Cabin" bill enabled a settler to claim 160 acres of land before it was offered publicly for sale, and later pay $1.25 an acre for it.

In 1842 Tyler did sign a tariff bill protecting northern manufacturers. The Webster-Ashburton treaty ended a Canadian boundary dispute; in 1845 Texas was annexed.

The administration of this states'-righter strengthened the Presidency. But it also increased sectional cleavage that led toward civil war. By the end of his term, Tyler had replaced the original Whig Cabinet with southern conservatives. In 1844 Calhoun became Secretary of State. Later these men returned to the Democratic Party, committed to the preservation of states' rights, planter interests, and the institution of slavery. Whigs became more representative of northern business and farming interests.

When the first southern states seceded in 1861, Tyler led a compromise movement; failing, he worked to create the Southern Confederacy. He died in 1862, a member of the Confederate House of Representatives.

At the end of John Tyler's administration, the United States annexed Texas.

James K. Polk

OFTEN REFERRED TO as the first "dark horse" President, James K. Polk was the last of the Jacksonians to sit in the White House, and the last strong President until the Civil War.

He was born in Mecklenburg County, North Carolina, in 1795. Studious and industrious, Polk was graduated with honors in 1818 from the University of North Carolina. As a young lawyer he entered politics, served in the Tennessee legislature, and became a friend of Andrew Jackson.

In the House of Representatives, Polk was a chief lieutenant of Jackson in his Bank war. He served as Speaker between 1835 and 1839, leaving to become Governor of Tennessee.

Until circumstances raised Polk's ambitions, he was a leading contender for the Democratic nomination for Vice President in 1844. Both Martin Van Buren, who had been expected to win the Democratic nomination for President, and Henry Clay, who was to be the Whig nominee, tried to take the expansionist issue out of the campaign by declaring themselves opposed to the annexation of Texas. Polk, however, publicly asserted that Texas should be "re-annexed" and all of Oregon "re-occupied."

The aged Jackson, correctly sensing that the people favored expansion, urged the choice of a candidate committed to the Nation's "Manifest Destiny." This view prevailed at the Democratic Convention, where Polk was nominated on the ninth ballot.

"Who is James K. Polk?" Whigs jeered. Democrats replied Polk was the candidate who stood for expansion. He linked the Texas issue, popular in the South, with the Oregon question, attractive to the North. Polk also favored acquiring California.

Even before he could take office, Congress passed a joint resolution offering annexation to Texas. In so doing they bequeathed Polk the possibility of war with Mexico, which soon severed diplomatic relations.

In his stand on Oregon, the President seemed to be risking war with Great Britain also. The 1844 Democratic platform claimed the entire Oregon area, from the California boundary northward to a latitude of 54°40′, the southern boundary of Russian Alaska. Extremists proclaimed "Fifty-four forty or fight," but Polk, aware of diplomatic realities, knew that no course short of war was likely to get all of Oregon. Happily, neither he nor the British wanted a war.

He offered to settle by extending the Canadian boundary, along the 49th parallel, from the Rockies to the Pacific. When the British minister declined, Polk reasserted the American claim to the entire area. Finally, the British settled for the 49th parallel, except for the southern tip of Vancouver Island. The treaty was signed in 1846.

Acquisition of California proved far more difficult. Polk sent an envoy to offer Mexico up to $20,000,000, plus settlement of damage claims owed to Americans, in return for California and the New Mexico country. Since no Mexican leader could cede half his country and still stay in power, Polk's envoy was not received. To bring pressure, Polk sent Gen. Zachary Taylor to the disputed area on the Rio Grande.

To Mexican troops this was aggression, and they attacked Taylor's forces.

Congress declared war and, despite much Northern opposition, supported the military operations. American forces won repeated victories and occupied Mexico City. Finally, in 1848, Mexico ceded New Mexico and California in return for $15,000,000 and American assumption of the damage claims.

President Polk added a vast area to the United States, but its acquisition precipitated a bitter quarrel between the North and the South over expansion of slavery.

Polk, leaving office with his health undermined from hard work, died in June 1849.

James K. Polk extended the Nation's boundaries to the shores of the Pacific.

Z. Taylor

TWELFTH PRESIDENT 1849-1850

NORTHERNERS and southerners disputed sharply whether the territories wrested from Mexico should be opened to slavery, and some southerners even threatened secession. Standing firm, Zachary Taylor was prepared to hold the Union together by armed force rather than by compromise.

Born in Virginia in 1784, he was taken as an infant to Kentucky and raised on a plantation. He was a career officer in the Army, but his talk was most often of cotton raising. His home was in Baton Rouge, Louisiana, and he owned a plantation in Mississippi.

But Taylor did not defend slavery or southern sectionalism; 40 years in the Army made him a strong nationalist.

He spent a quarter of a century policing the frontiers against Indians. In the Mexican War he won major victories at Monterrey and Buena Vista.

President Polk, disturbed by General Taylor's informal habits of command and perhaps his Whiggery as well, kept him in northern Mexico and sent an expedition under Gen. Winfield Scott to capture Mexico City. Taylor, incensed, thought that "the battle of Buena Vista opened the road to the city of Mexico and the halls of Montezuma, that others might revel in them."

"Old Rough and Ready's" homespun ways were political assets. His long military record would appeal to northerners; his ownership of 100 slaves would lure southern votes. He had not committed himself on troublesome issues. The Whigs nominated him to run against the Democratic candidate, Lewis Cass, who favored letting the residents of territories decide for themselves whether they wanted slavery.

In protest against Taylor the slaveholder and Cass the advocate of "squatter sovereignty," northerners who opposed extension of slavery into territories formed a Free Soil Party and nominated Martin Van Buren.

In a close election, the Free Soilers pulled enough votes away from Cass to elect Taylor.

Although Taylor had subscribed to Whig principles of legislative leadership, he was not inclined to be a puppet of Whig leaders in Congress. He acted at times as though he were above parties and politics.

As disheveled as always, Taylor tried to run his administration in the same rule-of-thumb fashion that he had fought Indians.

Traditionally, people could decide whether they wanted slavery when they drew up new state constitutions. Therefore, to end the dispute over slavery in new areas, Taylor urged settlers in New Mexico and California to draft constitutions and apply for statehood, bypassing the territorial stage.

Southerners were furious, since neither state constitution was likely to permit slavery; Members of Congress were dismayed, since they felt the President was usurping their policy-making prerogatives. In addition, Taylor's solution ignored several acute side issues: the northern dislike of the slave market operating in the District of Columbia; and the southern demands for a more stringent fugitive slave law.

In February 1850 President Taylor had held a stormy conference with southern leaders who threatened secession. He told them that if necessary to enforce the laws he personally would lead the Army. Persons "taken in rebellion against the Union, he would hang... with less reluctance than he had hanged deserters and spies in Mexico." He never wavered.

Then events took an unexpected turn. After participating in ceremonies at the Washington Monument on a blistering July 4, Taylor fell ill; within five days he was dead. After his death, the forces of compromise triumphed, but the war Taylor had been willing to face came 11 years later. In it, his only son Richard served as a general in the Confederate Army.

With Zachary Taylor, a career soldier first attained the Presidency.

Millard Fillmore

THIRTEENTH PRESIDENT 1850-1853

IN HIS RISE from a log cabin to wealth and the White House, Millard Fillmore demonstrated that through methodical industry and some competence an uninspiring man could make the American dream come true.

Born in the Finger Lakes country of New York in 1800, Fillmore as a youth endured the privations of frontier life. He worked on his father's farm, and at 15 was apprenticed to a cloth dresser. He attended one-room schools, and fell in love with the red-headed teacher, Abigail Powers, who later became his wife.

In 1823 he was admitted to the bar; seven years later he moved his law practice to Buffalo. As an associate of the Whig politician Thurlow Weed, Fillmore held state office and for eight years was a member of the House of Representatives. In 1848, while Comptroller of New York, he was elected Vice President.

Fillmore presided over the Senate during the months of nerve-wracking debates over the Compromise of 1850. He made no public comment on the merits of the compromise proposals, but a few days before President Taylor's death, he intimated to him that if there should be a tie vote on Henry Clay's bill, he would vote in favor of it.

Thus the sudden accession of Fillmore to the Presidency in July 1850 brought an abrupt political shift in the Administration. Taylor's Cabinet resigned and President Fillmore at once appointed Daniel Webster to be Secretary of State, thus proclaiming his alliance with the moderate Whigs who favored the Compromise.

A bill to admit California still aroused all the violent arguments for and against the extension of slavery, without any progress toward settling the major issues.

Clay, exhausted, left Washington to recuperate, throwing leadership upon Senator Stephen A. Douglas of Illinois. At this critical juncture, President Fillmore announced in favor of the Compromise. On August 6, 1850, he sent a message to Congress recommending that Texas be paid to abandon her claims to part of New Mexico.

This helped influence a critical number of northern Whigs in Congress away from their insistence upon the Wilmot Proviso—the stipulation that all land gained by the Mexican War must be closed to slavery.

Douglas's effective strategy in Congress combined with Fillmore's pressure from the White House to give impetus to the Compromise movement. Breaking up Clay's single legislative package, Douglas presented five separate bills to the Senate:

1. Admit California as a free state.
2. Settle the Texas boundary and compensate her.
3. Grant territorial status to New Mexico.
4. Place Federal officers at the disposal of slaveholders seeking fugitives.
5. Abolish the slave trade in the District of Columbia.

Each measure obtained a majority, and by September 20, President Fillmore had signed them into law. Webster wrote, "I can now sleep of nights."

Some of the more militant northern Whigs remained irreconcilable, refusing to forgive Fillmore for having signed the Fugitive Slave Act. They helped deprive him of the Presidential nomination in 1852.

Within a few years it was apparent that although the Compromise had been intended to settle the slavery controversy, it served rather as an uneasy sectional truce.

As the Whig Party disintegrated in the 1850's, Fillmore refused to join the Republican Party; but, instead, in 1856 accepted the nomination for President of the Know Nothing, or American, Party. Throughout the Civil War he opposed President Lincoln and during Reconstruction supported President Johnson. He died in 1874.

Millard Fillmore's conciliatory policies helped postpone the Civil War.

Franklin Pierce

FOURTEENTH PRESIDENT 1853-1857

FRANKLIN PIERCE became President at a time of apparent tranquillity. The United States, by virtue of the Compromise of 1850, seemed to have weathered its sectional storm. By pursuing the recommendations of southern advisers, Pierce—a New Englander—hoped to prevent still another outbreak of that storm. But his policies, far from preserving calm, hastened the disruption of the Union.

Born in Hillsborough, New Hampshire, in 1804, Pierce attended Bowdoin College. After graduation he studied law, then entered politics. At 24 he was elected to the New Hampshire legislature; two years later he became its Speaker. During the 1830's he went to Washington, first as a Representative, then as a Senator.

Pierce, after serving in the Mexican War, was proposed by New Hampshire friends for the Presidential nomination in 1852. At the Democratic Convention, the delegates agreed easily enough upon a platform pledging undeviating support of the Compromise of 1850 and hostility to any efforts to agitate the slavery question. But they balloted 48 times and eliminated all the well-known candidates before nominating Pierce, a true "dark horse."

Probably because the Democrats stood more firmly for the Compromise than the Whigs, and because Whig candidate Gen. Winfield Scott was suspect in the South, Pierce won with a narrow margin of popular votes.

Two months before he took office, he and his wife saw their eleven-year-old son killed when their train was wrecked. Grief-stricken, Pierce entered the Presidency nervously exhausted.

In his Inaugural he proclaimed an era of peace and prosperity at home, and vigor in relations with other nations. The United States might have to acquire additional possessions for the sake of its own security, he pointed out, and would not be deterred by "any timid forebodings of evil."

Pierce had only to make gestures toward expansion to excite the wrath of northerners, who accused him of acting as a cat's-paw of southerners eager to extend slavery into other areas. Therefore he aroused apprehension when he pressured Great Britain to relinquish its special interests along part of the Central American coast, and even more when he tried to persuade Spain to sell Cuba.

But the most violent renewal of the storm stemmed from the Kansas-Nebraska Act, which repealed the Missouri Compromise and reopened the question of slavery in the West. This measure, the handiwork of Senator Stephen A. Douglas, grew in part out of his desire to promote a railroad from Chicago to California through Nebraska. Already Secretary of War Jefferson Davis, advocate of a southern transcontinental route, had persuaded Pierce to send James Gadsden to Mexico to buy land for a southern railroad. He purchased the area now comprising southern Arizona and part of southern New Mexico for $10,000,000.

Douglas's proposal, to organize western territories through which a railroad might run, caused extreme trouble. Douglas provided in his bills that the residents of the new territories could decide the slavery question for themselves. The result was a rush into Kansas, as southerners and northerners vied for control of the territory. Shooting broke out, and "bleeding Kansas" became a prelude to the Civil War.

By the end of his administration, Pierce could claim "a peaceful condition of things in Kansas." But, to his disappointment, the Democrats refused to renominate him, turning to the less controversial Buchanan. Pierce returned to New Hampshire, leaving his successor to face the rising fury of the sectional whirlwind. He died in 1869.

Under Franklin Pierce, guerrilla raids in Kansas heralded the approach of civil war.

James Buchanan

FIFTEENTH PRESIDENT 1857-1861

TALL, STATELY, stiffly formal in the high stock he wore around his jowls, James Buchanan was the only President who never married.

Presiding over a rapidly dividing Nation, Buchanan grasped inadequately the political realities of the time. Relying on constitutional doctrines to close the widening rift over slavery, he failed to understand that the North would not accept constitutional arguments which favored the South. Nor could he realize how sectionalism had realigned political parties: the Democrats split; the Whigs were destroyed, giving rise to the Republicans.

Born into a well-to-do Pennsylvania family in 1791, Buchanan, a graduate of Dickinson College, was gifted as a debater and learned in the law.

He was elected five times to the House of Representatives; then, after an interlude as Minister to Russia, served for a decade in the Senate. He became Polk's Secretary of State and Pierce's Minister to Great Britain. Service abroad helped to bring him the Democratic nomination in 1856 because it had exempted him from involvement in bitter domestic controversies.

As President-elect, Buchanan thought the crisis would disappear if he maintained a sectional balance in his appointments and could persuade the people to accept constitutional law as the Supreme Court interpreted it. The Court was considering the legality of restricting slavery in the territories, and two justices hinted to Buchanan what the decision would be.

Thus, in his Inaugural the President referred to the territorial question as "happily, a matter of but little practical importance" since the Supreme Court was about to settle it "speedily and finally."

Two days later Chief Justice Roger B. Taney delivered the Dred Scott decision, asserting that Congress had no constitutional power to deprive persons of their property rights in slaves in the territories. Southerners were delighted, but the decision created a furor in the North.

Buchanan decided to end the troubles in Kansas by urging the admission of the territory as a slave state. Although he directed his Presidential authority to this goal, he further angered the Republicans and alienated members of his own party. Kansas remained a territory.

When Republicans won a plurality in the House in 1858, every significant bill they passed fell before southern votes in the Senate or a Presidential veto. The Federal Government reached a stalemate.

Sectional strife rose to such a pitch in 1860 that the Democratic Party split into northern and southern wings, each nominating its own candidate for the Presidency. Consequently, when the Republicans nominated Abraham Lincoln, it was a foregone conclusion that he would be elected even though his name appeared on no southern ballot. Rather than accept a Republican administration, the southern "fire-eaters" advocated secession.

President Buchanan, dismayed and hesitant, denied the legal right of states to secede but held that the Federal Government legally could not prevent them. He hoped for compromise, but secessionist leaders did not want compromise.

Then Buchanan took a more militant tack. As several Cabinet members resigned, he appointed northerners, and sent the *Star of the West* to carry reinforcements to Fort Sumter. On January 9, 1861, the vessel was fired upon and driven away.

Buchanan reverted to a policy of inactivity that continued until he left office. In March 1861 he retired to his Pennsylvania home Wheatland—where he died seven years later—leaving his successor to resolve the frightful issue facing the Nation.

James Buchanan groped for compromise as the South advanced toward secession.

Abraham Lincoln

SIXTEENTH PRESIDENT 1861-1865

ABRAHAM LINCOLN warned the South in his Inaugural Address: "In *your* hands, my dissatisfied fellow countrymen, and not in *mine,* is the momentous issue of civil war. The government will not assail *you.... You* have no oath registered in Heaven to destroy the government, while *I* shall have the most solemn one to 'preserve, protect and defend' it."

Lincoln thought secession illegal, and was willing to use force to defend Federal law and the Union. When Confederate batteries fired on Fort Sumter and forced its surrender, he called on the states for 75,000 volunteers. Four more slave states joined the Confederacy but four remained within the Union. The Civil War had begun.

The son of a Kentucky frontiersman, Lincoln had to struggle for a living and for learning. Five months before receiving his party's nomination for President, he sketched his life:

"I was born Feb. 12, 1809, in Hardin County, Kentucky. My parents were both born in Virginia, of undistinguished families —second families, perhaps I should say. My mother, who died in my tenth year, was of a family of the name of Hanks.... My father ...removed from Kentucky to ... Indiana, in my eighth year.... It was a wild region, with many bears and other wild animals still in the woods. There I grew up.... Of course when I came of age I did not know much. Still somehow, I could read, write, and cipher ... but that was all."

Lincoln made extraordinary efforts to attain knowledge while working on a farm, splitting rails for fences, and keeping store at New Salem, Illinois. He was a captain in the Black Hawk War, spent eight years in the Illinois legislature, and rode the circuit of courts for many years. His law partner said of him, "His ambition was a little engine that knew no rest."

He married Mary Todd, and they had four boys, only one of whom lived to maturity.

In 1858 Lincoln ran against Stephen A. Douglas for Senator. He lost the election, but in debating with Douglas he gained a national reputation that won him the Republican nomination for President in 1860.

As President, he built the Republican Party into a strong national organization. Further, he rallied most of the northern Democrats to the Union cause.

On January 1, 1863, he issued the Emancipation Proclamation that declared forever free those slaves within the Confederacy.

Lincoln never let the world forget that the Civil War involved an even larger issue. This he stated most movingly in dedicating the military cemetery at Gettysburg: "that we here highly resolve that these dead shall not have died in vain—that this nation, under God, shall have a new birth of freedom—and that government of the people, by the people, for the people, shall not perish from the earth."

Lincoln won re-election in 1864, as Union military triumphs heralded an end to the war. In his planning for peace, the President was flexible and generous, encouraging southerners to lay down their arms and join speedily in reunion.

The spirit that guided him was clearly that of his Second Inaugural Address, now inscribed on one wall of the Lincoln Memorial in Washington, D. C.:

"With malice toward none; with charity for all; with firmness in the right, as God gives us to see the right, let us strive on to finish the work we are in; to bind up the nation's wounds...."

On Good Friday, April 14, 1865, Lincoln was assassinated at Ford's Theatre in Washington by John Wilkes Booth, an actor, who somehow thought he was helping the South. The opposite was the result, for with Lincoln's death, the possibility of peace with magnanimity died.

Abhorring war, Abraham Lincoln accepted it as the only means to save the Union.

Andrew Johnson

SEVENTEENTH PRESIDENT 1865-1869

WITH THE ASSASSINATION of Lincoln, the Presidency fell upon an old-fashioned southern Jacksonian Democrat of pronounced states' rights views. Although an honest and honorable man, Andrew Johnson was one of the most unfortunate of Presidents. Arrayed against him were the Radical Republicans in Congress, brilliantly led and ruthless in their tactics. Johnson was no match for them.

Born in Raleigh, North Carolina, in 1808, Johnson grew up in poverty. He was apprenticed to a tailor as a boy, but ran away. He opened a tailor shop in Greeneville, Tennessee, married Eliza McCardle, and participated in debates at the local academy.

Entering politics, he became an adept stump speaker, championing the common man and vilifying the plantation aristocracy. As a Member of the House of Representatives and the Senate in the 1840's and '50's, he advocated a homestead bill to provide a free farm for the poor man.

During the secession crisis, Johnson remained in the Senate even when Tennessee seceded, which made him a hero in the North and a traitor in the eyes of most southerners. In 1862 President Lincoln appointed him Military Governor of Tennessee, and Johnson used the state as a laboratory for reconstruction. In 1864 the Republicans, contending that their National Union Party was for all loyal men, nominated Johnson, a southerner and a Democrat, for Vice President.

After Lincoln's death, President Johnson proceeded to reconstruct the former Confederate States while Congress was not in session in 1865. He pardoned all who would take an oath of allegiance, but required leaders and men of wealth to obtain special Presidential pardons.

By the time Congress met in December 1865, most southern states were reconstructed, slavery was being abolished, but "black codes" to regulate the freedmen were beginning to appear.

Radical Republicans in Congress moved vigorously to change Johnson's program. They gained the support of northerners who were dismayed to see southerners keeping many prewar leaders and imposing many prewar restrictions upon Negroes.

The Radicals' first step was to refuse to seat any Senator or Representative from the old Confederacy. Next they passed measures dealing with the former slaves. Johnson vetoed the legislation. The Radicals mustered enough votes in Congress to pass legislation over his veto—the first time that Congress had overridden a President on an important bill. They passed the Civil Rights Act of 1866, which established Negroes as American citizens and forbade discrimination against them.

A few months later Congress submitted to the states the Fourteenth Amendment, which specified that no state should "deprive any person of life, liberty, or property, without due process of law."

All the former Confederate States except Tennessee refused to ratify the amendment; further, there were two bloody race riots in the South. Speaking in the Middle West, Johnson faced hostile audiences. The Radical Republicans won an overwhelming victory in Congressional elections that fall.

In March 1867, the Radicals effected their own plan of Reconstruction, again placing southern states under military rule. They passed laws placing restrictions upon the President. When Johnson allegedly violated one of these, the Tenure of Office Act, by dismissing Secretary of War Edwin M. Stanton, the House voted eleven articles of impeachment against him. He was tried by the Senate in the spring of 1868 and acquitted by one vote.

In 1875, Tennessee returned Johnson to the Senate. He died a few months later.

Andrew Johnson faced impeachment for steadfastly opposing Radicals in Congress.

EIGHTEENTH PRESIDENT 1869/1877

L ATE in the administration of Andrew Johnson, Gen. Ulysses S. Grant quarreled with the President and aligned himself with the Radical Republicans. He was, as the symbol of Union victory during the Civil War, their logical candidate for President in 1868.

When he was elected, the American people hoped for an end to turmoil. Grant provided neither vigor nor reform. Looking to Congress for direction, he seemed bewildered. One visitor to the White House noted "a puzzled pathos, as of a man with a problem before him of which he does not understand the terms."

Born in 1822, Grant was the son of an Ohio tanner. He went to West Point rather against his will and graduated in the middle of his class. In the Mexican War he fought under Gen. Zachary Taylor.

At the outbreak of the Civil War, Grant was working in his father's leather store in Galena, Illinois. He was appointed by the Governor to command an unruly volunteer regiment. Grant whipped it into shape and by September 1861 he had risen to the rank of brigadier general of volunteers.

He sought to win control of the Mississippi Valley. In February 1862 he took Fort Henry and attacked Fort Donelson. When the Confederate commander asked for terms, Grant replied, "No terms except an unconditional and immediate surrender can be accepted." The Confederates surrendered, and President Lincoln promoted Grant to major general of volunteers.

At Shiloh in April, Grant fought one of the bloodiest battles in the West and came out less well. President Lincoln fended off demands for his removal by saying, "I can't spare this man—he fights."

For his next major objective, Grant maneuvered and fought skillfully to win Vicksburg, the key city on the Mississippi, and thus cut the Confederacy in two. Then he broke the Confederate hold on Chattanooga.

Lincoln appointed him General-in-Chief in March 1864. Grant directed Sherman to drive through the South while he himself, with the Army of the Potomac, pinned down Gen. Robert E. Lee's Army of Northern Virginia.

Finally, on April 9, 1865, at Appomattox Court House, Lee surrendered. Grant wrote out magnanimous terms of surrender that would prevent treason trials.

As President, Grant presided over the Government much as he had run the Army. Indeed he brought part of his Army staff to the White House.

Although a man of scrupulous honesty, Grant as President accepted handsome presents from admirers. Worse, he allowed himself to be seen with two speculators, Jay Gould and James Fisk. When Grant realized their scheme to corner the market in gold, he authorized the Secretary of the Treasury to sell enough gold to wreck their plans, but the speculation had already wrought havoc with business.

During his campaign for re-election in 1872, Grant was attacked by Liberal Republican reformers. He called them "narrow-headed men," their eyes so close together that "they can look out of the same gimlet hole without winking." The General's friends in the Republican Party came to be known proudly as "the Old Guard."

Grant allowed Radical Reconstruction to run its course in the South, bolstering it at times with military force.

After retiring from the Presidency, Grant became a partner in a financial firm, which went bankrupt. About that time he learned that he had cancer of the throat. He started writing his recollections to pay off his debts, racing against death to produce a memoir that ultimately earned nearly $450,000. Soon after completing the last page, in 1885, he died.

Gen. Ulysses S. Grant came to the Presidency a great military hero.

R B Hayes

NINETEENTH PRESIDENT 1877-1881

BENEFICIARY of the most fiercely disputed election in American history, Rutherford B. Hayes brought to the Executive Mansion dignity, honesty, and moderate reform.

To the delight of the Woman's Christian Temperance Union, Lucy Webb Hayes carried out her husband's orders to banish wines and liquors from the White House.

Born in Ohio in 1822, Hayes was educated at Kenyon College and Harvard Law School. After five years' law practice in Lower Sandusky, he moved to Cincinnati, where he flourished as a young Whig lawyer.

He fought in the Civil War, was wounded in action, and rose to the rank of brevet major general. While he was still in the Army, Cincinnati Republicans ran him for the House of Representatives. He accepted the nomination, but would not campaign, explaining, "an officer fit for duty who at this crisis would abandon his post to electioneer . . . ought to be scalped."

Elected by a heavy majority, Hayes entered Congress in December 1865, troubled by the "Rebel influences . . . ruling the White House." Between 1867 and 1876 he served three terms as Governor of Ohio.

Safe liberalism, party loyalty, and a good war record made Hayes an acceptable Republican candidate in 1876. He opposed Governor Samuel J. Tilden of New York.

Although a galaxy of famous Republican speakers, and even Mark Twain, stumped for Hayes, he expected the Democrats to win. When the first returns seemed to confirm this, Hayes went to bed, believing he had lost. But in New York, Republican National Chairman Zachariah Chandler, aware of a loophole, wired leaders to stand firm: "Hayes has 185 votes and is elected." The popular vote apparently was 4,300,000 for Tilden to 4,036,000 for Hayes. Hayes's election depended upon contested electoral votes in Louisiana, South Carolina, and Florida. If all the disputed electoral votes went to Hayes, he would win; a single one would elect Tilden.

Months of uncertainty followed. In January 1877 Congress established an Electoral Commission to decide the dispute. The commission, made up of eight Republicans and seven Democrats, determined all the contests in favor of Hayes by eight to seven. The final electoral vote: 185 to 184.

Northern Republicans had been promising southern Democrats at least one Cabinet post, Federal patronage, subsidies for internal improvements, and withdrawal of troops from Louisiana and South Carolina.

Hayes insisted that his appointments must be made on merit, not political considerations. For his Cabinet he chose men of high caliber, but outraged many Republicans because one member was an ex-Confederate and another had bolted the party as a Liberal Republican in 1872.

Hayes pledged protection of the rights of Negroes in the South, but at the same time advocated the restoration of "wise, honest, and peaceful local self-government." This meant the withdrawal of troops. Hayes hoped such conciliatory policies would lead to the building of a "new Republican party" in the South, to which white businessmen and conservatives would rally.

Many of the leaders of the new South did indeed favor Republican economic policies and approved of Hayes's financial conservatism, but they faced annihilation at the polls if they were to join the party of Reconstruction. Hayes and his Republican successors were persistent in their efforts but could not win over the "solid South."

Hayes had announced in advance that he would serve only one term, and retired to Spiegel Grove, his home in Fremont, Ohio, in 1881. He died in 1893.

Rutherford B. Hayes gained the Presidency by a margin of only one electoral vote.

James A. Garfield.

TWENTIETH PRESIDENT 1881

A S THE LAST of the log cabin Presidents, James A. Garfield attacked political corruption and won back for the Presidency a measure of prestige it had lost during the Reconstruction period.

He was born in Cuyahoga County, Ohio, in 1831. Fatherless at two, he later drove canal boat teams, somehow earning enough money for an education. He was graduated from Williams College in Massachusetts in 1856, and he returned to the Western Reserve Eclectic Institute (later Hiram College) in Ohio as a classics professor. Within a year he was made its president.

Garfield was elected to the Ohio Senate in 1859 as a Republican. During the secession crisis, he advocated coercing the seceding states back into the Union.

In 1862, when Union military victories had been few, he successfully led a brigade at Middle Creek, Kentucky, against Confederate troops. At 31, Garfield became a brigadier general, two years later a major general of volunteers.

Meanwhile, in 1862, Ohioans elected him to Congress. President Lincoln persuaded him to resign his commission: It was easier to find major generals than to obtain effective Republicans for Congress. Garfield repeatedly won re-election for 18 years, and became the leading Republican in the House.

At the 1880 Republican Convention, Garfield failed to win the Presidential nomination for his friend John Sherman. Finally, on the 36th ballot, Garfield himself became the "dark horse" nominee.

By a margin of only 10,000 popular votes, Garfield defeated the Democratic nominee, Gen. Winfield Scott Hancock.

As President, Garfield strengthened Federal authority over the New York Customs House, stronghold of Senator Roscoe Conkling, who was leader of the Stalwart Republicans and dispenser of patronage in New York. When Garfield submitted to the Senate a list of appointments including many of Conkling's friends, he named Conkling's arch-rival William H. Robertson to run the Customs House. Conkling contested the nomination, tried to persuade the Senate to block it, and appealed to the Republican caucus to compel its withdrawal.

But Garfield would not submit: "This ... will settle the question whether the President is registering clerk of the Senate or the Executive of the United States.... shall the principal port of entry ... be under the control of the administration or under the local control of a factional senator."

Conkling maneuvered to have the Senate confirm Garfield's uncontested nominations and adjourn without acting on Robertson. Garfield countered by withdrawing all nominations except Robertson's; the Senators would have to confirm him or sacrifice all the appointments of Conkling's friends.

In a final desperate move, Conkling and his fellow-Senator from New York resigned, confident that their legislature would vindicate their stand and re-elect them. Instead, the legislature elected two other men; the Senate confirmed Robertson. Garfield's victory was complete.

In foreign affairs, Garfield's Secretary of State invited all American republics to a conference to meet in Washington in 1882. But the conference never took place. On July 2, 1881, in a Washington railroad station, an embittered attorney who had sought a consular post shot the President.

Mortally wounded, Garfield lay in the White House for weeks. Alexander Graham Bell, inventor of the telephone, tried unsuccessfully to find the bullet with an induction balance electrical device which he had designed.

On September 6, Garfield was taken to the New Jersey seaside. He seemed to be recuperating, but on September 19, 1881, he died.

James A. Garfield died from an assassin's bullet only six months after he took office.

Chester A. Arthur

TWENTY-FIRST PRESIDENT 1881-1885

DIGNIFIED and handsome, with clean-shaven chin and sidewhiskers, Chester A. Arthur "looked like a President."

The son of a Baptist preacher who had emigrated from northern Ireland, Arthur was born in Fairfield, Vermont, in 1829. He was graduated from Union College in 1848, taught school, was admitted to the bar, and practiced law in New York City. Early in the Civil War he served as Quartermaster General of the State of New York.

President Grant in 1871 appointed him Collector of the Port of New York. Arthur effectively marshalled the thousand Customs House employees under his supervision on behalf of Roscoe Conkling's Stalwart Republican machine.

Honorable in his personal life and his public career, Arthur nevertheless was a firm believer in the spoils system when it was coming under vehement attack from reformers. He insisted upon honest administration of the Customs House, but staffed it with more employees than it needed, retaining them for their merit as party workers rather than as Government officials.

In 1878 President Hayes, attempting to reform the Customs House, ousted Arthur. Conkling and his followers tried to win redress by fighting for the renomination of Grant at the 1880 Republican Convention. Failing, they reluctantly accepted the nomination of Arthur for the Vice Presidency.

During his brief tenure as Vice President, Arthur stood firmly beside Conkling in his patronage struggle against President Garfield. But when Arthur succeeded to the Presidency, he was eager to prove himself above machine politics.

Avoiding old political friends, he became a man of fashion in his garb and associates, and often was seen with the élite of Washington, New York, and Newport. To the indignation of the Stalwart Republicans, the onetime Collector of the Port of New York became, as President, a champion of civil service reform. Public pressure, heightened by the assassination of Garfield, forced an unwieldy Congress to heed the President.

In 1883 Congress passed the Pendleton Act, which established a bipartisan Civil Service Commission, forbade levying political assessments against officeholders, and provided for a "classified system" that made certain Government positions obtainable only through competitive written examinations. The system protected employees against removal for political reasons.

Acting independently of party dogma, Arthur also tried to lower tariff rates so the Government would not be embarrassed by annual surpluses of revenue. Congress raised about as many rates as it trimmed, but Arthur signed the Tariff Act of 1883. Aggrieved westerners and southerners looked to the Democratic Party for redress, and the tariff began to emerge as a major political issue between the two parties.

The Arthur Administration enacted the first general Federal immigration law. Arthur approved a measure in 1882 excluding paupers, criminals, and lunatics. Congress suspended Chinese immigration for ten years, later making the restriction permanent.

Arthur demonstrated as President that he was above factions within the Republican Party, if indeed not above the party itself. Perhaps in part his reason was the well-kept secret he had known since a year after he succeeded to the Presidency, that he was suffering from a fatal kidney disease. He kept himself in the running for the Presidential nomination in 1884 in order not to appear that he feared defeat, but was not renominated, and died in 1886. Publisher Alexander K. McClure recalled, "No man ever entered the Presidency so profoundly and widely distrusted, and no one ever retired . . . more generally respected."

Chester A. Arthur, former machine politician, became a reformer in the Presidency.

Grover Cleveland

22D PRESIDENT 1885-1889, 24TH PRESIDENT 1893-1897

THE FIRST DEMOCRAT elected after the Civil War, Grover Cleveland was the only President to leave the White House and return for a second term four years later.

One of nine children of a Presbyterian minister, Cleveland was born in New Jersey in 1837. He was raised in upstate New York. As a lawyer in Buffalo, he became notable for his single-minded concentration upon whatever task faced him.

At 44, he emerged into a political prominence that carried him to the White House in three years. Running as a reformer, he was elected Mayor of Buffalo in 1881, and later, Governor of New York.

Cleveland won the Presidency with the combined support of Democrats and reform Republicans, the "Mugwumps," who disliked the record of his opponent James G. Blaine of Maine.

A bachelor, Cleveland was ill at ease at first with all the comforts of the White House. "I must go to dinner," he wrote a friend, "but I wish it was to eat a pickled herring a Swiss cheese and a chop at Louis' instead of the French stuff I shall find." In June 1886 Cleveland married 21-year-old Frances Folsom; he was the only President married in the White House.

Cleveland vigorously pursued a policy barring special favors to any economic group. Vetoing a bill to appropriate $10,000 to distribute seed grain among drought-stricken farmers in Texas, he wrote: "Federal aid in such cases encourages the expectation of paternal care on the part of the Government and weakens the sturdiness of our national character. . . ."

He also vetoed many private pension bills to Civil War veterans whose claims were fraudulent. When Congress, pressured by the Grand Army of the Republic, passed a bill granting pensions for disabilities not caused by military service, Cleveland vetoed it, too.

He angered the railroads by ordering an investigation of western lands they held by Government grant. He forced them to return 81,000,000 acres. He also signed the Interstate Commerce Act, the first law attempting Federal regulation of the railroads.

In December 1887 he called on Congress to reduce high protective tariffs. Told that he had given Republicans an effective issue for the campaign of 1888, he retorted, "What is the use of being elected or reelected unless you stand for something?" But Cleveland was defeated in 1888; although he won a larger popular majority than the Republican candidate Benjamin Harrison, he received fewer electoral votes.

Elected again in 1892, Cleveland faced an acute depression. He dealt directly with the Treasury crisis rather than with business failures, farm mortgage foreclosures, and unemployment. He obtained repeal of the mildly inflationary Sherman Silver Purchase Act and, with the aid of Wall Street, maintained the Treasury's gold reserve.

When railroad strikers in Chicago violated an injunction, Cleveland sent Federal troops to enforce it. "If it takes the entire army and navy of the United States to deliver a post card in Chicago," he thundered, "that card will be delivered."

Cleveland's blunt treatment of the railroad strikers stirred the pride of many Americans. So did the vigorous way in which he forced Great Britain to accept arbitration of a disputed boundary in Venezuela. But his policies during the depression were generally unpopular. His party deserted him and nominated William Jennings Bryan in 1896.

After leaving the White House, Cleveland lived in retirement in Princeton, New Jersey. He died in 1908.

Grover Cleveland was the only President elected to two nonconsecutive terms.

Benj Harrison

TWENTY-THIRD PRESIDENT 1889-1893

NOMINATED for President on the eighth ballot at the 1888 Republican Convention, Benjamin Harrison conducted one of the first "front-porch" campaigns, delivering short speeches to delegations that visited him in Indianapolis. As he was only 5 feet, 6 inches tall, Democrats called him "Little Ben"; Republicans replied that he was big enough to wear the hat of his grandfather, "Old Tippecanoe."

Born in 1833 on a farm by the Ohio River below Cincinnati, Harrison attended Miami University in Ohio and read law in Cincinnati. He moved to Indianapolis, where he practiced law and campaigned for the Republican Party. He married Caroline Lavinia Scott in 1853. After the Civil War —he was Colonel of the 70th Volunteer Infantry—Harrison became a pillar of Indianapolis, enhancing his reputation as a brilliant lawyer.

The Democrats defeated him for Governor of Ohio in 1876 by unfairly stigmatizing him as "Kid Gloves" Harrison. In the 1880's he served in the United States Senate, where he championed Indians, homesteaders, and Civil War veterans.

In the Presidential election, Harrison received 100,000 fewer popular votes than Cleveland, but carried the Electoral College 233 to 168. Although Harrison had made no political bargains, his supporters had given innumerable pledges upon his behalf.

When Boss Matt Quay of Pennsylvania heard that Harrison ascribed his narrow victory to Providence, Quay exclaimed that Harrison would never know "how close a number of men were compelled to approach ... the penitentiary to make him President."

Harrison was proud of the vigorous foreign policy which he helped shape. The first Pan American Congress met in Washington in 1889, establishing an information center which later became the Pan American Union. At the end of his administration Harrison submitted to the Senate a treaty to annex Hawaii; to his disappointment, President Cleveland later withdrew it.

Substantial appropriation bills were signed by Harrison for internal improvements, naval expansion, and subsidies for steamship lines. For the first time except in war, Congress appropriated a billion dollars. When critics attacked "the billion-dollar Congress," Speaker Thomas B. Reed replied, "This is a billion-dollar country." President Harrison also signed the Sherman Anti-Trust Act "to protect trade and commerce against unlawful restraints and monopolies," the first Federal act attempting to regulate trusts.

The most perplexing domestic problem Harrison faced was the tariff issue. The high tariff rates in effect had created a surplus of money in the Treasury. Low-tariff advocates argued that the surplus was hurting business. Republican leaders in Congress successfully met the challenge. Representative William McKinley and Senator Nelson W. Aldrich framed a still higher tariff bill; some rates were intentionally prohibitive.

Harrison tried to make the tariff more acceptable by writing in reciprocity provisions. To cope with the Treasury surplus, the tariff was removed from imported raw sugar; sugar growers within the United States were given two cents a pound bounty on their production.

Long before the end of the Harrison Administration, the Treasury surplus had evaporated, and prosperity seemed about to disappear as well. Congressional elections in 1890 went stingingly against the Republicans, and party leaders decided to abandon President Harrison although he had cooperated with Congress on party legislation. Nevertheless, his party renominated him in 1892, but he was defeated by Cleveland.

After he left office, Harrison returned to Indianapolis, and married the widowed Mrs. Mary Dimmick in 1896. A dignified elder statesman, he died in 1901.

Of Chief Executives, only Benjamin Harrison was the grandson of a President.

William McKinley

TWENTY-FIFTH PRESIDENT 1897-1901

AT THE 1896 Republican Convention, in time of depression, the wealthy Cleveland businessman Marcus Alonzo Hanna ensured the nomination of his friend William McKinley as "the advance agent of prosperity." The Democrats, advocating the "free and unlimited coinage of both silver and gold"—which would have mildly inflated the currency—nominated William Jennings Bryan.

While Hanna used large contributions from eastern Republicans frightened by Bryan's views on silver, McKinley met delegations on his front porch in Canton, Ohio. He won by the largest majority of popular votes since 1872.

Born in Niles, Ohio, in 1843, McKinley briefly attended Allegheny College, and was teaching in a country school when the Civil War broke out. Enlisting as a private in the Union Army, he was mustered out at the end of the war as a brevet major of volunteers. He studied law, opened an office in Canton, Ohio, and married Ida Saxton, daughter of a local banker.

At 34, McKinley won a seat in Congress. His attractive personality, exemplary character, and quick intelligence enabled him to rise rapidly. He was appointed to the powerful Ways and Means Committee. Robert M. La Follette, Sr., who served with him, recalled that he generally "represented the newer view," and "on the great new questions . . . was generally on the side of the public and against private interests."

During his 14 years in the House, he became the leading Republican tariff expert, giving his name to the measure enacted in 1890. The next year he was elected Governor of Ohio, serving two terms.

When McKinley became President, the depression of 1893 had almost run its course and with it the extreme agitation over silver. Deferring action on the money question, he called Congress into special session to enact the highest tariff in history.

In the friendly atmosphere of the McKinley Administration, industrial combinations developed at an unprecedented pace. Newspapers caricatured McKinley as a little boy led around by "Nursie" Hanna, the representative of the trusts. However, McKinley was not dominated by Hanna; he condemned the trusts as "dangerous conspiracies against the public good."

Not prosperity, but foreign policy, dominated McKinley's Administration. Reporting the stalemate between Spanish forces and revolutionaries in Cuba, newspapers screamed that a quarter of the population was dead and the rest suffering acutely. Public indignation brought pressure upon the President for war. Unable to restrain Congress or the American people, McKinley delivered his message of neutral intervention in April 1898. Congress thereupon voted three resolutions tantamount to a declaration of war for the liberation and independence of Cuba.

In the 100-day war, the United States destroyed the Spanish fleet outside Santiago harbor in Cuba, seized Manila in the Philippines, and occupied Puerto Rico.

"Uncle Joe" Cannon, later Speaker of the House, once said that McKinley kept his ear so close to the ground that it was full of grasshoppers. When McKinley was undecided what to do about Spanish possessions other than Cuba, he toured the country and detected an imperialist sentiment. Thus the United States annexed the Philippines, Guam, and Puerto Rico.

In 1900, McKinley again campaigned against Bryan. While Bryan inveighed against imperialism, McKinley quietly stood for "the full dinner pail."

His second term, which had begun auspiciously, came to a tragic end in September 1901. He was standing in a receiving line at the Buffalo Pan-American Exposition when a deranged anarchist shot him twice. He died eight days later.

Under William McKinley the Nation gained its first overseas possessions.

Theodore Roosevelt

TWENTY-SIXTH PRESIDENT 1901-1909

WITH THE ASSASSINATION of President McKinley, Theodore Roosevelt, not quite 43, became the youngest President in the Nation's history. He brought new excitement and power to the Presidency, as he vigorously led Congress and the American public toward progressive reforms and a strong foreign policy.

He took the view that the President as a "steward of the people" should take whatever action necessary for the public good unless expressly forbidden by law or the Constitution. "I did not usurp power," he wrote, "but I did greatly broaden the use of executive power."

Roosevelt's youth differed sharply from that of the log cabin Presidents. He was born in New York City in 1858 into a wealthy family, but he too struggled—against ill health—and in his triumph became an advocate of the strenuous life.

In 1884 his first wife, Alice Lee Roosevelt, and his mother died on the same day. Roosevelt spent much of the next two years on his ranch in the Badlands of Dakota Territory. There he mastered his sorrow as he lived in the saddle, driving cattle, hunting big game—he even captured an outlaw. On a visit to London, he married Edith Carow in December 1886.

During the Spanish-American War, Roosevelt was lieutenant colonel of the Rough Rider Regiment, which he led on a charge at the battle of San Juan. He was one of the most conspicuous heroes of the war.

Boss Tom Platt, needing a hero to draw attention away from scandals in New York State, accepted Roosevelt as the Republican candidate for Governor in 1898. Roosevelt won and served with distinction.

As President, Roosevelt held the ideal that the Government should be the great arbiter of the conflicting economic forces in the Nation, especially between capital and labor, guaranteeing justice to each and dispensing favors to none.

Roosevelt emerged spectacularly as a "trust buster" by forcing the dissolution of a great railroad combination in the Northwest. Other antitrust suits under the Sherman Act followed.

Roosevelt steered the United States more actively into world politics. He liked to quote a favorite proverb, "Speak softly and carry a big stick. . . ."

Aware of the strategic need for a short cut between the Atlantic and Pacific, Roosevelt ensured the construction of the Panama Canal. His corollary to the Monroe Doctrine prevented the establishment of foreign bases in the Caribbean and arrogated the sole right of intervention in Latin America to the United States.

He won the Nobel Peace Prize for mediating the Russo-Japanese War, reached a Gentleman's Agreement on immigration with Japan, and sent the Great White Fleet on a goodwill tour of the world.

Some of Roosevelt's most effective achievements were in conservation. He added enormously to the national forests in the West, reserved lands for public use, and fostered great irrigation projects.

He crusaded endlessly on matters big and small, exciting audiences with his high-pitched voice, jutting jaw, and pounding fist. "The life of strenuous endeavor" was a must for those around him, as he romped with his five younger children and led ambassadors on hikes through Rock Creek Park in Washington, D. C.

Leaving the Presidency in 1909, Roosevelt went on an African safari, then jumped back into politics. In 1912 he ran for President on a Progressive ticket. To reporters he once remarked that he felt as fit as a bull moose, the name of his new party.

While campaigning in Milwaukee, he was shot in the chest by a fanatic. Roosevelt soon recovered, but his words at that time would have been applicable at the time of his death in 1919: "No man has had a happier life than I have led; a happier life in every way."

Theodore Roosevelt, nature lover and conservationist, championed the strenuous life.

TWENTY-SEVENTH PRESIDENT 1909-1913

DISTINGUISHED JURIST, effective administrator, but poor politician, William Howard Taft spent four uncomfortable years in the White House. Large, jovial, conscientious, he was caught in the intense battles between progressives and conservatives, and got scant credit for the achievements of his administration.

Born in 1857, the son of a distinguished judge, he was graduated from Yale, and returned to Cincinnati to study and practice law. He rose in politics through Republican judiciary appointments, through his own competence and availability, and because, as he once wrote facetiously, he always had his "plate the right side up when offices were falling."

But Taft much preferred law to politics. He was appointed a Federal circuit judge at 34. He aspired to be a member of the Supreme Court, but his wife, Helen Herron Taft, held other ambitions for him.

His route to the White House was via administrative posts. President McKinley sent him to the Philippines in 1900 as chief civil administrator. Sympathetic toward the Filipinos, he improved the economy, built roads and schools, and gave the people at least some participation in government.

President Roosevelt made him Secretary of War, and by 1907 had decided that Taft should be his successor. The Republican Convention nominated him the next year.

Taft disliked the campaign—"one of the most uncomfortable four months of my life." But he pledged his fealty to the Roosevelt program, popular in the West, while his brother Charles reassured eastern Republicans. William Jennings Bryan, running on the Democratic ticket for a third time, complained that he was having to oppose two candidates, a western progressive Taft and an eastern conservative Taft.

Progressives were pleased with Taft's election. "Roosevelt has cut enough hay," they said; "Taft is the man to put it into the barn." Conservatives were delighted to be rid of Roosevelt—the "mad messiah."

Taft recognized that his techniques would differ from those of his predecessor. Unlike Roosevelt, Taft did not believe in the stretching of Presidential powers. He once commented that Roosevelt "ought more often to have admitted the legal way of reaching the same ends."

Taft alienated many liberal Republicans who later formed the Progressive Party, by defending the Payne-Aldrich Act which unexpectedly continued high tariff rates. A trade agreement with Canada, which Taft pushed through Congress, would have pleased eastern advocates of a low tariff, but the Canadians rejected it. He further antagonized progressives by upholding his Secretary of the Interior, accused of failing to carry out Roosevelt's conservation policies.

In the angry Progressive onslaught against him, little attention was paid to the fact that his administration initiated 80 antitrust suits and that Congress submitted to the states amendments for a Federal income tax and the direct election of Senators. A postal savings system was established, and the Interstate Commerce Commission was directed to set railroad rates.

In 1912, when the Republicans renominated Taft, Roosevelt bolted the party to lead the Progressives, thus guaranteeing the election of Woodrow Wilson.

Taft, free of the Presidency, served as Professor of Law at Yale until President Harding made him Chief Justice of the United States, a position he held until just before his death in 1930. To Taft, the appointment was his greatest honor; he wrote: "I don't remember that I ever was President."

William Howard Taft: the only man to become President and then Chief Justice.

58

TWENTY-EIGHTH PRESIDENT 1913-1921

LIKE ROOSEVELT before him, Woodrow Wilson regarded himself as the personal representative of the people. "No one but the President," he said, "seems to be expected . . . to look out for the general interests of the country." He developed a program of progressive reform and asserted international leadership in building a new world order. In 1917 he proclaimed American entrance into World War I a crusade to make the world "safe for democracy."

Wilson had seen the frightfulness of war. He was born in Virginia in 1856, the son of a Presbyterian minister who during the Civil War was a pastor in Augusta, Georgia, and during Reconstruction a professor in the charred city of Columbia, South Carolina.

After graduation from Princeton (then the College of New Jersey) and the University of Virginia Law School, Wilson earned his doctorate at Johns Hopkins University and entered upon an academic career. In 1885 he married Ellen Louise Axson.

Wilson advanced rapidly as a conservative young professor of political science and became president of Princeton in 1902.

His growing national reputation led some conservative Democrats to consider him Presidential timber. First they persuaded him to run for Governor of New Jersey in 1910. In the campaign he asserted his independence of the conservatives and of the machine that had nominated him, endorsing a progressive platform, which he pursued as Governor.

He was nominated for President at the 1912 Democratic Convention and campaigned on a program called the New Freedom, which stressed individualism and states' rights. In the three-way election he received only 42 percent of the popular vote but an overwhelming electoral vote.

Wilson maneuvered through Congress three major pieces of legislation. The first was a lower tariff, the Underwood Act; attached to the measure was a graduated Federal income tax. The passage of the Federal Reserve Act provided the Nation with the more elastic money supply it badly needed. In 1914 antitrust legislation established a Federal Trade Commission to prohibit unfair business practices.

Another burst of legislation followed in 1916. One new law prohibited child labor; another limited railroad workers to an eight-hour day. By virtue of this legislation and the slogan "he kept us out of war," Wilson narrowly won re-election.

But after the election Wilson concluded that America could not remain neutral in the World War. On April 2, 1917, he asked Congress for a declaration of war on Germany.

Massive American effort slowly tipped the balance in favor of the Allies. Wilson went before Congress in January 1918, to enunciate American war aims—the Fourteen Points, the last of which would establish "A general association of nations . . . affording mutual guarantees of political independence and territorial integrity to great and small states alike."

After the Germans signed the Armistice in November 1918, Wilson went to Paris to try to build an enduring peace. He later presented to the Senate the Versailles Treaty, containing the Covenant of the League of Nations, and asked, "Dare we reject it and break the heart of the world?"

But the election of 1918 had shifted the balance in Congress to the Republicans. By seven votes the Versailles Treaty failed in the Senate.

The President, against the warnings of his doctors, had made a national tour to mobilize public sentiment for the treaty. Exhausted, he suffered a stroke and nearly died. Tenderly nursed by his second wife, Edith Bolling Galt, he lived until 1924.

Woodrow Wilson tried in vain to bring the United States into the League of Nations.

Warren G. Harding [signature]

TWENTY-NINTH PRESIDENT 1921-1923

BEFORE his nomination, Warren G. Harding declared, "America's present need is not heroics, but healing; not nostrums, but normalcy; not revolution, but restoration; not agitation, but adjustment; not surgery, but serenity; not the dramatic, but the dispassionate; not experiment, but equipoise; not submergence in internationality, but sustainment in triumphant nationality...."

A Democratic leader, William Gibbs McAdoo, called Harding's speeches "an army of pompous phrases moving across the landscape in search of an idea." Their very murkiness was effective, since Harding's pronouncements remained unclear on the League of Nations, in contrast to the impassioned crusade of the Democratic candidates, Governor James M. Cox of Ohio and Franklin D. Roosevelt.

Thirty-one distinguished Republicans had signed a manifesto assuring voters that a vote for Harding was a vote for the League. But Harding interpreted his election as a mandate to stay out of the League of Nations.

Harding, born near Marion, Ohio, in 1865, became the publisher of a newspaper. He married a divorcee, Mrs. Florence Kling De Wolfe. He was a trustee of the Trinity Baptist Church, a director of almost every important business, and a leader in fraternal organizations and charitable enterprises. He organized the Citizens' Cornet Band, available for both Republican and Democratic rallies; "I played every instrument but the slide trombone and the E-flat cornet," he once remarked.

Harding's undeviating Republicanism and vibrant speaking voice, plus his willingness to let the machine bosses set policies, led him far in Ohio politics. He served in the state Senate and as Lieutenant Governor, and unsuccessfully ran for Governor. He delivered the nominating address for President Taft at the 1912 Republican Conven-

tion. In 1914 he was elected to the Senate, which he found "a very pleasant place."

An Ohio admirer, Harry Daugherty, began to promote Harding for the 1920 Republican nomination because, as he later explained, "He looked like a President."

Thus a group of Senators, taking control of the 1920 Republican Convention when the principal candidates deadlocked, turned to Harding. He won the Presidential election by an unprecedented landslide of 60 percent of the popular vote.

Republicans in Congress easily got the President's signature on their bills. They eliminated wartime controls and slashed taxes, established a Federal budget system, restored the high protective tariff, and imposed tight limitations upon immigration.

By 1923 the postwar depression seemed to be giving way to a new surge of prosperity, and newspapers hailed Harding as a wise statesman carrying out his campaign promise—"Less government in business and more business in government."

Behind the façade, not all of Harding's Administration was so impressive. Word began to reach the President that some of his friends were using their official positions for their own enrichment. Alarmed, he complained, "My ... friends ... they're the ones that keep me walking the floors nights!"

Looking wan and depressed, Harding journeyed westward in the summer of 1923, taking with him his upright Secretary of Commerce, Herbert Hoover. "If you knew of a great scandal in our administration," he asked Hoover, "would you for the good of the country and the party expose it publicly or would you bury it?" Hoover urged publishing it, but Harding feared the political repercussions.

He did not live to find out how the public would react to the scandals of his administration. In August 1923, he died in San Francisco of a heart attack.

Winner by a landslide, Warren G. Harding, friends said, "looked like a President."

THIRTIETH PRESIDENT 1923-1929

AT 2:30 on the morning of August 3, 1923, while visiting in Vermont, Calvin Coolidge received word that he was President. By the light of a kerosene lamp, his father, who was a notary public, administered the oath of office as Coolidge placed his hand on the family Bible.

Coolidge was "distinguished for character more than for heroic achievement," wrote a Democratic admirer, Alfred E. Smith. "His great task was to restore the dignity and prestige of the Presidency when it had reached the lowest ebb in our history . . . in a time of extravagance and waste. . . ."

Born at Plymouth, Vermont, on July 4, 1872, Coolidge was the son of a village storekeeper. He was graduated from Amherst College with honors, and entered law and politics in Northampton, Massachusetts. Slowly, methodically, he went up the political ladder from councilman in Northampton to Governor of Massachusetts, as a Republican. En route he became thoroughly conservative.

As President, Coolidge demonstrated his determination to preserve the old moral and economic precepts amid the material prosperity which many Americans were enjoying. He refused to use Federal economic power to check the growing boom or to ameliorate the depressed condition of agriculture and certain industries. His first message to Congress in December 1923 called for isolation in foreign policy, and for tax cuts, economy, and limited aid to farmers.

He rapidly became popular. In 1924, as the beneficiary of what was becoming known as "Coolidge prosperity," he polled more than 54 percent of the popular vote.

In his Inaugural he asserted that the country had achieved "a state of contentment seldom before seen," and pledged himself to maintain the status quo. In subsequent years he twice vetoed farm relief bills, and killed a plan to produce cheap Federal electric power on the Tennessee River.

The political genius of President Coolidge, Walter Lippmann pointed out in 1926, was his talent for effectively doing nothing: "This active inactivity suits the mood and certain of the needs of the country admirably. It suits all the business interests which want to be let alone. . . . And it suits all those who have become convinced that government in this country has become dangerously complicated and top-heavy. . . ."

Coolidge was both the most negative and remote of Presidents, and the most accessible. He once explained to Bernard Baruch why he often sat silently through interviews: "Well, Baruch, many times I say only 'yes' or 'no' to people. Even that is too much. It winds them up for twenty minutes more."

But no President was kinder in permitting himself to be photographed in Indian war bonnets or cowboy dress, and in greeting a variety of delegations to the White House.

Both his dry Yankee wit and his frugality with words became legendary. His gracious and lovely wife, Grace Goodhue Coolidge, recounted that a young woman sitting next to Coolidge at a dinner party confided to him she had bet she could engage him in conversation for five minutes. Without looking at her he quietly retorted, "You lose." And in 1928, while vacationing in the Black Hills of South Dakota, he issued the most famous of his laconic statements, "I do not choose to run for President in 1928."

By the time the disaster of the Great Depression hit the country, Coolidge was in retirement. Before his death in January, 1933, he confided to an old friend, ". . . I feel I no longer fit in with these times."

Laconic New Englander Calvin Coolidge strongly favored frugality in government.

Herbert Hoover

THIRTY-FIRST PRESIDENT 1929-1933

SON of a Quaker blacksmith, Herbert Hoover brought to the Presidency an unparalleled reputation for public service as an engineer, administrator, and humanitarian.

Born in an Iowa village in 1874, he grew up in Oregon. He enrolled at Stanford University when it opened in 1891, graduating as a mining engineer.

He married his Stanford sweetheart, Lou Henry, and they went to China, where he worked for a private corporation as China's leading engineer. In June 1900 the Boxer Rebellion caught the Hoovers in Tientsin. For almost a month the settlement was under heavy fire. While his wife worked in the hospitals, Hoover directed the building of barricades, and once risked his life rescuing Chinese children.

One week before Hoover celebrated his 40th birthday in London, Germany declared war on France, and the American Consul General asked his help in getting stranded tourists home. In six weeks his committee helped 120,000 Americans return to the United States. Next Hoover turned to a far more difficult task, to feed Belgium, which had been overrun by the German army.

After the United States entered the war, President Wilson appointed Hoover head of the Food Administration. He succeeded in cutting consumption of foods needed overseas and avoided rationing at home, yet kept the Allies fed.

After the Armistice, Hoover, a member of the Supreme Economic Council and head of the American Relief Administration, organized shipments of food for starving millions in central Europe. He extended aid to famine-stricken Soviet Russia in 1921. When a critic inquired if he was not thus helping Bolshevism, Hoover retorted, "Twenty million people are starving. Whatever their politics, they shall be fed!"

After capably serving as Secretary of Commerce under Presidents Harding and Coolidge, Hoover became the Republican Presidential nominee in 1928. He said then: "We in America today are nearer to the final triumph over poverty than ever before in the history of any land." His election seemed to ensure prosperity. Yet within months the stock market crashed, and the Nation spiraled downward into depression.

After the crash Hoover announced that while he would keep the Federal budget balanced, he would cut taxes and expand public works spending.

In 1931 repercussions from Europe deepened the crisis, even though the President presented to Congress a program asking for creation of the Reconstruction Finance Corporation to aid business, additional help for farmers facing mortgage foreclosures, banking reform, a loan to states for feeding the unemployed, expansion of public works, and drastic governmental economy.

At the same time he reiterated his view that while people must not suffer from hunger and cold, caring for them must be primarily a local and voluntary responsibility.

His opponents in Congress, who he felt were sabotaging his program for their own political gain, unfairly painted him as a callous and cruel President. Hoover became the scapegoat for the depression and was badly defeated in 1932. In the 1930's he became a powerful critic of the New Deal, warning against tendencies toward statism.

In 1947 President Truman appointed Hoover to a commission, which elected him chairman, to reorganize the Executive Departments. He was appointed chairman of a similar commission by President Eisenhower in 1953. Many economies resulted from both commissions' recommendations. Over the years, Hoover wrote many articles and books, one of which he was working on when he died in New York City, October 20, 1964.

Herbert Hoover's record of service abroad and at home spanned half a century.

Franklin D Roosevelt (signature)

THIRTY-SECOND PRESIDENT 1933-1945

ASSUMING THE PRESIDENCY at the depth of the Great Depression, Franklin D. Roosevelt helped the American people regain faith in themselves. He brought hope as he promised prompt, vigorous action, and asserted in his Inaugural Address, "the only thing we have to fear is fear itself."

Born in 1882 at Hyde Park, New York—now a national historic site—he attended Harvard University and Columbia Law School. On St. Patrick's Day, 1905, he married Eleanor Roosevelt.

Following the example of his fifth cousin, President Theodore Roosevelt, whom he greatly admired, Franklin D. Roosevelt entered public service through politics, but as a Democrat. He won election to the New York Senate in 1910. President Wilson appointed him Assistant Secretary of the Navy, and he was the Democratic nominee for Vice President in 1920.

In the summer of 1921, when he was 39, disaster hit—he was stricken with poliomyelitis. Demonstrating indomitable courage, he fought to regain the use of his legs, particularly through swimming. At the 1924 Democratic Convention he dramatically appeared on crutches to nominate Alfred E. Smith as "the Happy Warrior." In 1928 Roosevelt became Governor of New York.

He was elected President in November 1932, to the first of four terms. By March there were 13,000,000 unemployed, and almost every bank was closed. In his first "hundred days," he proposed, and Congress enacted, a sweeping program to bring recovery to business and agriculture, relief to the unemployed and to those in danger of losing farms and homes, and reform, especially through the establishment of the Tennessee Valley Authority.

By 1935 the Nation had achieved some measure of recovery, but businessmen and bankers were turning more and more against Roosevelt's New Deal program. They feared his experiments, were appalled because he had taken the Nation off the gold standard and allowed deficits in the budget, and disliked the concessions to labor. Roosevelt responded with a new program of reform: Social Security, heavier taxes on the wealthy, new controls over banks and public utilities, and an enormous work relief program for the unemployed.

In 1936 he was re-elected by a top-heavy margin. Feeling he was armed with a popular mandate, he sought legislation to enlarge the Supreme Court, which had been invalidating key New Deal measures. Roosevelt lost the Supreme Court battle, but a revolution in constitutional law took place. Thereafter the Government could legally regulate the economy.

Roosevelt had pledged the United States to the "good neighbor" policy, transforming the Monroe Doctrine from a unilateral American manifesto into arrangements for mutual action against aggressors. He also sought through neutrality legislation to keep the United States out of the war in Europe, yet at the same time to strengthen nations threatened or attacked. When France fell and England came under siege in 1940, he began to send Great Britain all possible aid short of actual military involvement.

When the Japanese attacked Pearl Harbor on December 7, 1941, Roosevelt directed organization of the Nation's manpower and resources for global war.

Feeling that the future peace of the world would depend upon relations between the United States and Russia, he devoted much thought to the planning of a United Nations, in which, he hoped, international difficulties could be settled.

As the war drew to a close, Roosevelt's health deteriorated, and on April 12, 1945, while at Warm Springs, Georgia, he died of a cerebral hemorrhage.

Franklin D. Roosevelt led the Nation through its worst depression and greatest war.

THIRTY-THIRD PRESIDENT 1945-1953

DURING HIS FEW WEEKS as Vice President, Harry S Truman scarcely saw President Roosevelt, and received no briefing on the development of the atomic bomb or the unfolding difficulties with Soviet Russia. Suddenly these and a host of other wartime problems became Truman's to solve when, on April 12, 1945, he became President. He told reporters, "I felt like the moon, the stars, and all the planets had fallen on me."

Truman was born in Lamar, Missouri, in 1884. He grew up in Independence, and for 12 years prospered as a Missouri farmer.

He went to France during World War I as a captain in the Field Artillery. Returning, he married Elizabeth Virginia Wallace, and opened a haberdashery in Kansas City.

Active in the Democratic Party, Truman was elected a judge of the Jackson County Court (an administrative position) in 1922. He became a Senator in 1934. During World War II he headed the Senate war investigating committee, checking into waste and corruption and saving perhaps as much as fifteen billion dollars.

As President, Truman made some of the most crucial decisions in history. Soon after V-E Day, the war against Japan had reached its final stage. An urgent plea to Japan to surrender was rejected. Truman, after consultations with his advisers, ordered atomic bombs dropped on cities devoted to war work. Two were Hiroshima and Nagasaki. Japanese surrender quickly followed.

In June 1945 Truman witnessed the signing of the charter of the United Nations, hopefully established to preserve peace.

Thus far, he had followed his predecessor's policies, but he soon developed his own. He presented to Congress a 21-point program, proposing the expansion of Social Security, a full employment program, a per-manent Fair Employment Practices Act, public housing and slum clearance. The program, Truman wrote, "symbolizes for me my assumption of the office of President in my own right." It became known as the Fair Deal.

Dangers and crises marked the foreign scene as Truman campaigned successfully in 1948. In foreign affairs he was already providing his most effective leadership.

In 1947 as the Soviet Union pressured Turkey and, through guerrillas, threatened to take over Greece, he asked Congress to aid the two countries, enunciating the program that bears his name—the Truman Doctrine. The Marshall Plan, named for his Secretary of State, stimulated spectacular economic recovery in war-torn western Europe.

When the Russians blockaded the western sectors of Berlin in 1948, Truman created a massive airlift to supply Berliners until the Russians backed down. Meanwhile, he was negotiating a military alliance to protect Western nations, the North Atlantic Treaty Organization, established in 1949.

In June 1950, when the Communist government of North Korea attacked South Korea, Truman conferred promptly with his military advisers. There was, he wrote, "complete, almost unspoken acceptance on the part of everyone that whatever had to be done to meet this aggression had to be done. There was no suggestion from anyone that either the United Nations or the United States could back away from it."

A long, discouraging struggle ensued as U.N. forces held a line above the old boundary of South Korea. Truman kept the war a limited one, rather than risk a major conflict with China and perhaps Russia.

Deciding not to run again, he retired to Independence; at age 88, he died December 26, 1972, after a stubborn fight for life.

For Harry S Truman, war and cold war posed challenges unprecedented in history.

Dwight D Eisenhower

THIRTY-FOURTH PRESIDENT 1953-1961

BRINGING to the Presidency his prestige as commanding general of the victorious forces in Europe during World War II, Dwight D. Eisenhower obtained a truce in Korea and worked incessantly during his two terms to ease the tensions of the cold war. He pursued the moderate policies of "Modern Republicanism," pointing out as he left office, "America is today the strongest, the most influential, and most productive nation in the world."

Born in Texas in 1890, brought up in Abilene, Kansas, Eisenhower was the third of seven sons. He excelled in sports in high school, and received an appointment to West Point. Stationed in Texas as a second lieutenant, he met Mamie Geneva Doud, whom he married in 1916.

In his early Army career, he excelled in staff assignments, serving under Generals John J. Pershing, Douglas MacArthur, and Walter Krueger. After Pearl Harbor, General George C. Marshall called him to Washington for a war plans assignment. He commanded the Allied Forces landing in North Africa in November 1942; on D-Day, 1944, he was Supreme Commander of the troops invading France.

After the war, he became President of Columbia University, then took leave to assume supreme command over the new NATO forces being assembled in 1951. Republican emissaries to his headquarters near Paris persuaded him to run for President in 1952.

"I like Ike" was an irresistible slogan; Eisenhower won a sweeping victory.

Negotiating from military strength, he tried to reduce the strains of the cold war. In 1953, the signing of a truce brought an armed peace along the border of South Korea. The death of Stalin the same year caused shifts in relations with Russia.

New Russian leaders consented to a peace treaty neutralizing Austria. Meanwhile, both Russia and the United States had developed hydrogen bombs. With the threat of such destructive force hanging over the world, Eisenhower, with the leaders of the British, French, and Russian governments, met at Geneva in July 1955.

The President proposed that the United States and Russia exchange blueprints of each other's military establishments and "provide within our countries facilities for aerial photography to the other country." The Russians greeted the proposal with silence, but were so cordial throughout the meetings that tensions relaxed.

Suddenly, in September 1955, Eisenhower suffered a heart attack in Denver, Colorado. After seven weeks he left the hospital, and in February 1956 doctors reported his recovery. In November he was elected for his second term.

In domestic policy the President pursued a middle course, continuing most of the New Deal and Fair Deal programs, emphasizing a balanced budget. As desegregation of schools began, he sent troops into Little Rock, Arkansas, to assure compliance with the orders of a Federal court; he also ordered the complete desegregation of the Armed Forces. "There must be no second class citizens in this country," he wrote.

Eisenhower concentrated on maintaining world peace. He watched with pleasure the development of his "atoms for peace" program—the loan of American uranium to "have not" nations for peaceful purposes.

Before he left office in January 1961, for his farm in Gettysburg, he urged the necessity of maintaining an adequate military strength, but cautioned that vast, long-continued military expenditures could breed potential dangers to our way of life. He concluded with a prayer for peace "in the goodness of time." Both themes remained timely and urgent when he died, after long illness, on March 28, 1969.

War hero Dwight D. Eisenhower proclaimed the Nation's desire for world peace.

THIRTY-FIFTH PRESIDENT 1961-1963

O N NOVEMBER 22, 1963, when he was hardly past his first thousand days in office, John Fitzgerald Kennedy was killed by an assassin's bullets as his motorcade wound through Dallas, Texas. Kennedy was the youngest man elected President; he was the youngest to die.

Of Irish descent, he was born in Brookline, Massachusetts, on May 29, 1917. Graduating from Harvard in 1940, he entered the Navy. In 1943, when his PT boat was rammed and sunk by a Japanese destroyer, Kennedy, despite grave injuries, led the survivors through perilous waters to safety.

Back from the war, he became a Democratic Congressman from the Boston area, advancing in 1953 to the Senate. He married Jacqueline Bouvier on September 12, 1953. In 1955, while recuperating from a back operation, he wrote *Profiles in Courage,* which won the Pulitzer Prize in history.

In 1956 Kennedy almost gained the Democratic nomination for Vice President, and four years later was a first-ballot nominee for President. Millions watched his television debates with the Republican candidate, Richard M. Nixon. Winning by a narrow margin in the popular vote, Kennedy became the first Roman Catholic President.

His Inaugural Address offered the memorable injunction: "Ask not what your country can do for you—ask what you can do for your country." As President, he set out to redeem his campaign pledge to get America moving again. His economic programs launched the country on its longest sustained expansion since World War II; before his death, he laid plans for a massive assault on persisting pockets of privation and poverty.

Responding to ever more urgent demands, he took vigorous action in the cause of equal rights, calling for new civil rights legislation. His vision of America extended to the quality of the national culture and the central role of the arts in a vital society.

He wished America to resume its old mission as the first nation dedicated to the revolution of human rights. With the Alliance for Progress and the Peace Corps, he brought American idealism to the aid of developing nations. But the hard reality of the Communist challenge remained.

Shortly after his inauguration, Kennedy permitted a band of Cuban exiles, already armed and trained, to invade their homeland. The attempt to overthrow the regime of Fidel Castro was a failure. Soon thereafter, the Soviet Union renewed its campaign against West Berlin. Kennedy replied by reinforcing the Berlin garrison and increasing the Nation's military strength, including new efforts in outer space. Confronted by this reaction, Moscow, after the erection of the Berlin Wall, relaxed its pressure in central Europe.

Instead, the Russians now sought to install nuclear missiles in Cuba. When this was discovered by air reconnaissance in October 1962, Kennedy imposed a quarantine on all offensive weapons bound for Cuba. While the world trembled on the brink of nuclear war, the Russians backed down and agreed to take the missiles away. The American response to the Cuban crisis evidently persuaded Moscow of the futility of nuclear blackmail.

Kennedy now contended that both sides had a vital interest in stopping the spread of nuclear weapons and slowing the arms race —a contention which led to the test ban treaty of 1963. The months after the Cuban crisis showed significant progress toward his goal of "a world of law and free choice, banishing the world of war and coercion." His administration thus saw the beginning of new hope for both the equal rights of Americans and the peace of the world.

John F. Kennedy: the youngest man elected President, the youngest to die in office.

"A GREAT SOCIETY" for the American people and their fellow men elsewhere was the vision of Lyndon B. Johnson. In his first years of office he obtained passage of one of the most extensive legislative programs in the Nation's history. Maintaining collective security, he carried on the rapidly growing struggle to restrain Communist encroachment in Viet Nam.

Johnson was born on August 27, 1908, in southwest Texas, not far from Johnson City, which his family had helped settle. He felt the pinch of rural poverty as he grew up, working his way through Southwest Texas State Teachers College; he learned compassion for the poverty of others when he taught students of Mexican descent.

In 1937 he campaigned successfully for the House of Representatives on a New Deal platform, effectively aided by his wife, the former Claudia "Lady Bird" Taylor, whom he had married in 1934.

During World War II he served briefly in the Navy as a lieutenant commander, winning a Silver Star in the South Pacific.

After six terms in the House, Johnson was elected to the Senate in 1948. In 1953, he became the youngest Minority Leader in Senate history, and the following year, when the Democrats won control, Majority Leader. With rare skill he obtained passage of a number of key Eisenhower measures.

In the 1960 campaign, Johnson, as John F. Kennedy's running mate, was elected Vice President. On November 22, 1963, when Kennedy was assassinated, Johnson was sworn in as President.

First he obtained enactment of the measures President Kennedy had been urging at the time of his death—a new civil rights bill and a tax cut. Next he urged the Nation "to build a great society, a place where the meaning of man's life matches the marvels of man's labor." In 1964, Johnson won the Presidency with 61 percent of the vote and had the widest popular margin in American history—more than 15,000,000 votes.

The Great Society program became Johnson's agenda for Congress in January 1965: aid to education, attack on disease, Medicare, urban renewal, beautification, conservation, development of depressed regions, a wide-scale fight against poverty, control and prevention of crime and delinquency, removal of obstacles to the right to vote. Congress, at times augmenting or amending, rapidly enacted Johnson's recommendations. Millions of elderly people found succor through the 1965 Medicare amendment to the Social Security Act.

Under Johnson, the country made spectacular explorations of space in a program he had championed since its start. When three astronauts successfully orbited the moon in December 1968, Johnson congratulated them: "You've taken . . . all of us, all over the world, into a new era. . . ."

Nevertheless, two overriding crises had been gaining momentum since 1965. Despite the beginning of new anti-poverty and anti-discrimination programs, unrest and rioting in black ghettos troubled the Nation. President Johnson steadily exerted his influence against segregation and on behalf of law and order, but there was no early solution.

The other crisis arose from Viet Nam. Despite Johnson's efforts to end Communist aggression and achieve a settlement, fighting continued. Controversy over the war had become acute by the end of March 1968, when he limited the bombing of North Viet Nam in order to initiate negotiations. At the same time, he startled the world by withdrawing as a candidate for re-election so that he might devote his full efforts, unimpeded by politics, to the quest for peace.

When he left office, peace talks were under way; he did not live to see them successful, but died suddenly of a heart attack at his Texas ranch on January 22, 1973.

Lyndon B. Johnson worked unceasingly toward a Great Society for the Nation.

Richard Nixon

THIRTY-SEVENTH PRESIDENT 1969-1974

RECONCILIATION was the first goal set by President Richard M. Nixon. The Nation was painfully divided, with turbulence in the cities and war overseas. During his Presidency, Nixon succeeded in ending American fighting in Viet Nam and improving relations with the U.S.S.R. and China. But the Watergate scandal brought fresh divisions to the country and led ultimately to his resignation.

His election in 1968 climaxed a career unusual both for his early success and for his comeback after being defeated for President in 1960 and for Governor of California in 1962.

Born in California in 1913, Nixon had a brilliant record at Whittier College and Duke University Law School before beginning the practice of law. In 1940, he married Patricia Ryan; they have two daughters, Patricia and Julie. During World War II, Nixon served as a Navy lieutenant commander in the Pacific.

On leaving the service, he was elected to Congress from his California district. In 1950, he won a Senate seat. Two years later, General Eisenhower selected Nixon, age 39, to be his running mate.

As Vice President, Nixon performed significant duties in the Eisenhower Administration. He was nominated for President by acclamation in 1960, but lost by a narrow margin to John F. Kennedy. He continued to campaign for other Republicans. In 1968, he again won his party's nomination, and went on to defeat Vice President Hubert H. Humphrey and third-party candidate George C. Wallace.

In his first term, he proposed reforms in such areas as welfare, tax laws, and the structure of the Government. His accomplishments while in office included revenue sharing, the end of the draft, new anti-crime laws, and a broad environmental program. As he had promised, he appointed Justices of conservative philosophy to the Supreme Court. One of the most dramatic events of his first term occurred in 1969, when American astronauts made the first moon landing.

Some of his most acclaimed achievements came in his quest for world stability. During visits in 1972 to Peking and Moscow, he reduced tensions with China and the U.S.S.R. His summit meetings with Russian leader Leonid I. Brezhnev produced a treaty to limit strategic nuclear weapons. In January 1973, he announced an accord with North Viet Nam to end American involvement in Indochina. In 1974, his Secretary of State, Henry Kissinger, negotiated disengagement agreements between Israel and its opponents, Egypt and Syria.

In 1972, Nixon defeated Democrat George McGovern by one of the widest margins on record.

Within a few months, his Administration was embattled over the so-called "Watergate" scandal, stemming from a break-in at the offices of the Democratic National Committee during the 1972 campaign. The break-in was traced to officials of the Committee to Re-elect the President. A number of Administration officials resigned; some were later convicted of offenses connected with efforts to cover up the affair. Nixon denied any personal involvement, but the courts forced him to yield tape recordings which indicated that he had, in fact, tried to divert the investigation.

As a result of unrelated scandals in Maryland, Vice President Spiro T. Agnew resigned in 1973. Nixon nominated, and Congress approved, House Minority Leader Gerald R. Ford as Vice President.

Faced with what seemed almost certain impeachment, Nixon announced on August 8, 1974, that he would resign the next day to begin "that process of healing which is so desperately needed in America."

The Watergate scandal forced Richard M. Nixon to resign the Presidency.

Gerald R. Ford

THIRTY-EIGHTH PRESIDENT 1974-

When Gerald R. Ford took the oath of office on August 9, 1974, he declared, "I assume the Presidency under extraordinary circumstances.... This is an hour of history that troubles our minds and hurts our hearts."

It was indeed an unprecedented time. He had been the first Vice President chosen under the terms of the Twenty-fifth Amendment, and in the aftermath of the Watergate scandal, was succeeding the first President ever to resign.

Ford was confronted with almost insuperable tasks. There were the challenges of mastering inflation, reviving a depressed economy, solving chronic energy shortages, and trying to ensure world peace.

The President acted to curb the trend toward government intervention and spending as a means of solving the problems of American society and the economy. In the long run, he believed this shift would bring a better life for all Americans.

Ford's reputation for integrity and openness had made him popular during his twenty-five years in Congress. From 1965 to 1973, he was House Minority Leader. Born in Omaha, Nebraska, in 1913, he grew up in Grand Rapids, Michigan. He starred on the University of Michigan football team, then went to Yale, where he served as assistant coach while earning his law degree. During World War II he attained the rank of lieutenant commander in the Navy. After the war he returned to Grand Rapids, where he began the practice of law, and entered Republican politics. A few weeks before his election to Congress in 1948, he married Elizabeth Bloomer. They have four children: Michael, John, Steven, and Susan.

As President, Ford tried to calm earlier controversies by granting former President Nixon a full pardon. His nominee for Vice President, former Governor Nelson Rockefeller of New York, was the second person to fill that office by appointment. Grad-

ually, Ford selected a cabinet of his own.

Ford established his policies during his first year in office, despite opposition from a heavily Democratic Congress. His first goal was to curb inflation. Then, when recession became the Nation's most serious domestic problem, he shifted to measures aimed at stimulating the economy. But, still fearing inflation, Ford vetoed a number of non-military appropriation bills that would further increase the already heavy budgetary deficit. During his first fourteen months as President he vetoed 39 measures. His vetoes were usually sustained.

Ford continued as he had in his Congressional days to view himself as "a moderate in domestic affairs, a conservative in fiscal affairs, and a dyed-in-the-wool internationalist in foreign affairs." A major goal was to help business operate more freely by reducing taxes upon it and easing the controls exercised by regulatory agencies. "We... declared our independence 200 years ago, and we are not about to lose it now to paper shufflers and computers," he said.

In foreign affairs Ford acted vigorously to maintain U. S. power and prestige after the collapse of Cambodia and South Viet Nam. Preventing a new war in the Middle East remained a major objective; by providing aid to both Israel and Egypt, the Ford Administration helped persuade the two countries to accept an interim truce agreement. Detente with the Soviet Union continued. President Ford and Soviet leader Leonid I. Brezhnev set new limitations upon nuclear weapons.

While debate continued over some of President Ford's policies, most Americans were in agreement on his high character, phenomenal energy, and warm accessibility. Twice within seventeen days in 1975 attempts were made upon his life. Both times he demonstrated courage under extreme stress. By his personal example he did much to restore confidence in the Presidency.

Gerald R. Ford set out to restore confidence in the Presidency

Index

JIMMY CARTER

A biographical supplement to the book

THE PRESIDENTS

OF THE UNITED STATES OF AMERICA

Published by the WHITE HOUSE HISTORICAL ASSOCIATION
with the cooperation of the NATIONAL GEOGRAPHIC SOCIETY, Washington, D. C.

Jimmy Carter (signature)

THIRTY-NINTH PRESIDENT 1977-

JIMMY CARTER aspired to make government "competent and compassionate," responsive to the American people and their expectations.

Carter—who has rarely used his full name—James Earl Carter, Jr.—was born on October 1, 1924, in Plains, Georgia. Peanut farming, talk of politics, and devotion to the Baptist faith were three mainstays of Carter's upbringing. "We felt close to nature," he has written, "close to the members of our family, and close to God."

After high school he attended junior college for a year, went on to Georgia Tech, then entered the Naval Academy at Annapolis, Maryland, as a sophomore. He was graduated in 1946, fifty-ninth in a class of 820. He did graduate work at Union College in Schenectady, New York, in 1952.

Carter married Rosalynn Smith, also from Plains, in 1946. He then began his first Navy assignment as an ensign at Norfolk, Virginia. The Carters have three sons, John William (Jack), James Earl III (Chip), Donnel Jeffrey (Jeff), and a daughter, Amy Lynn.

In 1948, Capt. Hyman Rickover accepted Carter in the nuclear submarine program, and made a profound impression on the young ensign. After he had served in the Navy seven years, his father died, and Lt. Carter resigned his commission and returned to Plains.

He entered state politics in 1962, and was elected to the Georgia Senate. Four years later, he lost in the Democratic gubernatorial primary by 20,000 votes; within a month he was campaigning again. By election day of 1970, Carter had given 1,800 speeches, and he and Rosalynn had shaken the hands of more than 600,000

people—and he was elected governor.

Among the new young southern governors, Carter attracted attention by emphasizing ecology, efficiency in government, and the erasing of racial barriers.

Carter announced his candidacy for President in December 1974 and began a two-year campaign. At first he attracted relatively little public attention, but gradually he won support. At the Democratic convention, he was nominated on the first ballot. He chose Senator Walter F. Mondale of Minnesota as his running mate.

He campaigned hard against President Gerald R. Ford, debating with him three times on television. Carter won with 50.1 percent of the popular vote, by 297 electoral votes to 241 for Ford.

After his inauguration, Jimmy and Rosalynn promptly broke precedent by walking, hand in hand, down Pennsylvania Avenue in the inaugural parade. Actions such as this boosted Carter's popularity and helped him obtain public support essential to his complex programs.

His major effort was to combat the continuing economic woes of stagnation, inflation, and unemployment. Carter proposed a 31-billion-dollar "stimulus package" for the economy with special emphasis on youth employment programs.

In foreign affairs, Carter again set his own style. His insistence upon championing the human rights of dissidents throughout the world was coldly received by the Soviet Union and some other governments.

Summarizing these developments after Carter's first hundred days in office, one analyst said of the President: "Conservatives find him less radical than they feared; liberals less militant than they hoped."

Jimmy Carter championed human rights throughout the world.

PRESS OF JUDD AND DETWEILER, INC., WASHINGTON, D. C.
COLOR PLATES BY J. WILLIAM REED CO., ALEXANDRIA, VIRGINIA
AND COLORGRAPHICS, INC., BELTSVILLE, MARYLAND